THE ROOTS OF WISDOM

THE ROOTS OF WISDOM
慧根

Selected Poetry of

Zang Di
臧棣

Translated from the Chinese by **Eleanor Goodman**

Zephyr Press
Brookline, Mass

Book design by *type*slowly
Printed in Michigan by Cushing-Malloy

The translator and poet are grateful for the month they spent together
at the Vermont Studio Center on a Luce Fellowship.

Zephyr Press acknowledges with gratitude the financial support
of the Massachusetts Cultural Council, the National Endowment for the Arts

masscutluralcouncil.org

ART WORKS.
arts.gov

and the Chinese Writers Association Translation Fund.

Zephyr Press, a non-profit arts and education 501(c)(3) organization,
publishes literary titles that foster a deeper understanding of cultures
and languages. Zephyr Press books are distributed to the trade in the U.S.
and Canada by Consortium Book Sales and Distribution [www.cbsd.com].

Cataloguing-in publication data is available from the Library of Congress.

ZEPHYR PRESS
www.zephyrpress.org

CONTENTS

Translator's Foreword

Longtime readers of Zang Di would be likely to agree on three points: he is startlingly prolific; his work is difficult; and he is one of the most influential poets writing in China today.

Zang Di's influence is seen not only in his poetry but also in his trenchant criticism; in both, he approaches topics from contemporary poetics to classical Chinese poetry to Western writers such as Rilke and Seamus Heaney. He has read and traveled widely, and it shows throughout his work. Many of the poems in this book were written "away"—away from home, away from familiar literary or philosophical traditions, away from well-trodden routes of thought. He includes a host of classical Chinese quotes and idioms, as well as ideas gleaned from extensive reading and travels through Europe, the US, Japan, Taiwan, South America, and beyond. Yet like Williams and his dictum of "no ideas but in things," Zang Di's most potent tactic is to show us the ordinary objects of the world, revolve them into a labyrinth of connections, and spread it all out to expose something unexpected.

Zang Di himself has lived through several distinct and unexpected historical eras. Born in Beijing in 1964, he experienced the Cultural Revolution firsthand as a child, and then as a teenager found himself in the midst of the subsequent cultural and economic opening up. He was a college student at Peking University, where he now teaches, during the heady days of the 1980s, when writers and artists were finding their feet in the twentieth century. At the same time, China was flooded with Western literature, art, pop culture, philosophy, and the trappings of modern life. In the fourteen years Zang Di spent at Peking University as a student—from entering the college in 1983 to graduating with a Ph.D. in 1997—China experienced breakneck growth, and social and political changes on an enormous scale. While much of this is palpable in Zang Di's poetry, he is more concerned with relative constants: diverse elements of the natural world, human psychology, love and its dissolution, language itself.

"First and foremost, writing poetry is a kind of work"

For more than a decade, Zang Di has persevered in the habit of writing a poem a day. This lends his verse a linguistic and thematic continuity, a unity of intention, and a sense of one intense intellect at work on an overarching task. This is by no means to say that his poetry is all alike: the poems vary in subject matter, tone, and gravity. Yet Zang Di's work is recognizable and undeniably his own; his style and the particular movement of the poem on the page mark his work unmistakably.

Part of this is his method of titling poems. Most of the poems in this book—selected largely, though not exclusively, from his 2011 collection *The Roots of Wisdom Series*—include the word "Series" in their title. He also favors "Association" and, more recently, "Primer." These markers serve both as an organizational structure and private game. While many poets of roughly his generation—most notably Bai Hua and Ouyang Jianghe—have turned to the epic poem to express this new century's discontents and triumphs, Zang Di's poems tend toward one standard length: half a page to a page, occasionally a bit longer or shorter. By connecting these poems, their topics, and the objects in them, however, Zang Di creates an extended masterwork of interwoven constituent parts. He perceives his poetry not only as work, that is, a job, but also as a life's work: it is what he will leave for future generations. The seemingly disconnected subjects of the 'Series' poems, ranging from honeysuckle to human nature to contemporary poetics to primitive man to "an anti-universe experience," all come together in a mutable constellation of contemporary experience. Unlike the epic poem, which is fixed in a particular configuration, these poems can be read in a different order each time, and thereby constitute something akin to life as it is lived. The objects, experiences, and mental processes that make up each day and year do not come in a set order, but rather combine and recombine to new effect within the context of any given life. Nevertheless, they are all still inextricably interwoven, and this is the way these poems should be read as well.

Another aspect of Zang Di's work in poetry and his commitment to the field—as he points to in the previous quote, which is taken from a 2017 interview—is his literary criticism and support of younger poets. He is known as a stern, sometimes implacable critic of that which he deems unworthy of attention, and a strong advocate for those he feels are taking Chinese poetry in fruitful directions. As a professor at Peking University, he routinely comes into contact with some of the brightest stars of tomorrow's poetry world, and has had a role in encouraging and guiding them. In both his criticism and poetry, he has helped to shape some of the major debates that have divided the poetry scene in China at different moments, in particular the questions of how much influence non-Chinese literature should have on contemporary poetry in Chinese, and how closely poetry should hew to ordinary experience. Zang Di has been central to the conversation around what contemporary Chinese poetry is and should be, no insignificant task to undertake.

This emphasis on work is also crucial in a social moment in which cultural production is taken less seriously than either physical or economic production. Factories are important, money-making businesses are important, putting food on the table is important. But poetry? To the minds of many in today's China (as in the United States, it bears pointing out), poetry is a product of the past or the pastime of a wastrel. In his poem commemorating Seamus Heaney, written in the fall of 2013 just after Heaney's death, Zang Di presses the point:

> As for the hole left by the digging, only sweat
> can fill it. Only this kind of hole
> leads to a deeper trust in this difficult world.
> > "After the Society for New Wisdom Association"

He picks up Heaney's metaphor from his famous manifesto poem "Digging," ("Between my finger and my thumb / The squat pen rests. / I'll dig with it.") and adds the sweat of labor, and the holes left in the earth after the harvest. The labor of the pen leads to its own harvests, and the punctures it can make in one's ordinary perceptions. One's day-to-day insensitivity or blindness result in a new appreciation of what there is to perceive if one only were to look.

"Poetry is a kind of slowness"

It may come as something of a surprise for a poet as prolific as Zang Di to talk about poetry as slowness. But what does he mean by it?

> You understand dampness,
>
> just as nature understands poetry. In Taipei I wanted to say
> that poetry is a kind of slowness. A simple example is
> dampness is also a kind of slowness.
> "In Taipei Series"

The body knows dampness as nature knows poetry, which is to say that the body is in large part made of water and comes from water, just as poetry is inherent in the minute patterns that underpin the natural world: patterns of sound, visual repetition, symmetry, and all manner of aesthetic experience. But to approach any of this, one must slow the continual processes of the conscious mind in order to reach toward that which is hidden within and beyond it. Writing poetry is a conscious activity, but it is also a subconscious one. As Joan Didion elegantly puts it: "I write entirely to find out what I'm thinking, what I'm looking at, what I see and what it means." The same is true for Zang Di, and frequently his poems follow just this process of discovery:

> Halfway up the mountain, a brief happiness
> floats in like mist. Mt. Wanren tries to catch up
> to the mountain falcon's pitch. He appears seven times.
> His perfect spirals come closer and closer
> to a response to life. That is indeed

a starting point, and in midair, he starts to seize
the most opportune moments. He isn't picky about his goal,
doesn't care if the field mouse or hare is worthy
of his surprise attack. As soon as he determines the optimum angle,
he begins to dive, giving death
an absolute velocity. The performance is repeated countless times,
but none of his prey knows what to call
the ending. This temporary happiness conflicts
with the fact that only I know how to define this ending.

"An Anti-Universe Experience Series"

First, there is the feeling of happiness, and then the object of the bird, representing the closed ecological system of the mountain. Next comes the specificity of the number of appearances, and the "perfect spirals" of the falcon's flight. The poet looks at the falcon, but also sees the bird's potential prey below. In the midst of the "performance," only the poet as observer is aware of the larger enactment—that of the inevitable death of all composite beings, himself among them. There is power in the naming—being able to "define this ending"—but also the profound powerlessness in realizing that all of our definitions and reasoning do not protect us from our ultimate end. This is "what it means" in Didion's formulation, and the art of the poem is the powerful movement from observation to epiphany.

This whole process takes time: the time to experience, to feel, to intuit, to write. The raw materials must be digested before they can appear as realization, either in the form of the poet putting words on the page or in the form of the reader coming to his or her own insights. Zang Di seeds the discovery, and urges the reader to give it time enough to grow. In his best poetry, he employs all the richness and complexity of his language to make the reader pause, encourage her to read and reread, until meaning begins to filter through. Zang Di's poetry cannot be read quickly, and it always resists easy understanding. It enacts its own guiding ethos: here, poetry can be nothing but slow.

Zang Di has only one master, and that is the language of poetry and its boundaries, which he seems ever determined to push. His juxtaposition of words and seeds leads to lush new landscapes of his own making, a world in which nature and the entirely manmade artifact of language merge and bear offspring. His materials are abundant:

> I have so much to work on,
> and so little to serve.
> I use the clouds to work, and icebergs, and rainbows,
> the bigger the raw material, the more exciting the space.
>
> With the new moon, I work late into a dark heart.
> But I serve only poetry, juxtaposing words and seeds.
> I use a mirror like a sieve,
> and along with practice come the tricks of the trade.
> "Imagine Seeds Never Die Series"

He mixes the fanciful (icebergs and rainbows) with the every day (clouds and the moon and mirrors) to refine an art particular to himself. This is the formation of the poet's voice, and, as with all great poets, his is a voice that is not only immediately recognizable as belonging to himself alone, but also is one that can speak to a multitude of experience. He does not shy away from current events and scandals: "poisoned milk powder," "ordinary corruption," "well-known brainwashing" all figure in his work. The heart of his project is not there, however, but in the "golden secrets" of the natural and human psychological worlds:

> When I lower my head, I see only these chrysanthemums,
> golden guides, the little hands curve up and out, like the cirrus
> of mollusks.
> A careless glance composes them into bright yellow petals.

And right now, I am being as careful as a broken string.
Raised this well, they surely understand politics,
and so, the civility of plants shows something profound about
    the universe.
                    "Golden Secret Series"

To the poet's eye, the natural world is a cipher not only for itself, but for the universe as a whole. Here we are privy to the poet's thought process: the flowers reach out like hands, or the marine tendril equivalent; their restraint, their very thingness, is a key to understanding the interactions between the political and the universal. For Zang Di, these leaps are instinctive, and the connections intuitive. Only to the careless—or the uninitiated—do the petals appear just as petals.

A rose is a rose is a rose, but for Zang Di plants and animals with all their physicality are also a way into human psychology, politics, and relationships. He is an acute observer of inner and outer worlds, and again and again finds intimate and surprising ways of connecting the two. This is perhaps Zang Di's greatest talent, and it is how he builds a complete world in his verse.

"Riddles have always refused their own style"

A rose may be a rose, but one can argue endlessly about whether *meigui* in Chinese is the same as "rose" in English. Of course it isn't! But yes, in the end, it comes close enough. Every translator confronts this riddle each time she sits down to do her work. She confronts it, or she carefully sets it aside for a day when she is not translating, because the question only gets in the way of the work. Zang Di's poetry was a joy to translate; it was also sometimes a nightmare. So much must be left behind, and an entirely new linguistic, cultural, and poetic context brought in; interpretations, and sometimes heavy-handed ones with all their intrinsic dangers, are necessary because ambiguity is inherent to Zang Di's style. As he puts it:

"The more abstract / the fire of reality, the more it's worth as medicine." But the translator must grasp onto something to bring these lines over into English, and that involves decisions, judgments, and leaps of faith. To do so, I have made every attempt to maintain the rhythms, line breaks, creative syntax, and wordplay of the original. When that failed in English, I have pushed the translation a bit farther from the original to capture what I take to be the overriding movement of the poem. Each poem is its own riddle; in a new language, every aspect of style must be refused, yet somehow in each successful translation the original riddle remains.

The work presented here in no way represents the arc of Zang Di's writing career, nor his stylistic breadth. These poems constitute an idiosyncratic selection based on my own reading and the poet's suggestions, spanning a recent and short range from 2011 to 2016. Rather than being representative, I believe they show Zang Di at his strongest and thus far most mature. He has embraced his role as an "intellectual" poet (as opposed to a "folk" or "popular" poet), and makes use of a diverse and rich range of literary and observed resources. This is the work of a poet at the height of his powers, writing with the full knowledge of what is at stake. I hope readers will slow down long enough to let the poems speak.

Eleanor Goodman

THE ROOTS OF WISDOM

新生丛书

两个我，闪过同一个瞬间。
紫燕，流萤，不相信梦里的小山谷
会输给记忆中的铁栅栏。
会不会飞并不重要，愿不愿飞
才是一种尺度。抖动的羽毛
感慨时间从不会出大错，算准了
随时都会有两个我。而离别的意味
只意味着离别还能意味着什么！
两个我，就像一对黑白翅膀。
而生活更像是一条线索。一松手，
世界比泥鳅还要滑。可以抓紧的东西
最后都爱上了落叶的轨迹。
金黄的我，醒目于过去的我很大，
但现在的我则无所谓大小。
小嫩芽的小招呼，胜过一切手段。
宇宙自有份量，不上虚无的当
就好比没必要把死亡看得太透。
赤裸的我曾令任何人都看不透，
它就做得很棒，它守住了我们的一个瞬间。
对时间来说，赤裸的我无足轻重，
但对记忆来说，它是留给形象的最后的机会。
而死亡不过是一条还没上钩的鱼。
只要有新生，现场就比春天的风还大。

New Life Series

Two selves flashing through the same brief moment.
Purple martins and fireflies don't believe the little valleys of dreams
will be defeated by fences of memory.
Whether one flies isn't important, whether one wants to fly
is a kind of measure. Shuddering feathers
never mistake time, calculating correctly
that at any given time there are two selves. But parting
only implies that parting has an implication!
Two selves like a pair of black and white wings.
But life is more like a clue. If one's grip loosens,
the world turns slipperier than a mudfish. Things that can be grasped
will ultimately fall in love with the orbit of falling leaves.
The golden self is more dazzlingly huge than the old self,
but now I care nothing for size.
The little greetings of tender seedlings surpass all artifice.
The universe has its own weight, and not being fooled by nothingness
is like not needing to see death too clearly.
The naked self was once opaque to everyone,
it did very well, it held onto our brief moment.
To time, the naked self is inconsequential,
but to memory, it is the last chance left to form.
Death is merely a fish not yet on the hook.
As long as there is new life, the present is larger than a spring breeze.

金色的秘密丛书

低头时，我只看见这菊花，
金色向导，小小的手臂曲张着，像软体动物的触须。
粗心看，才貌合成艳黄的花瓣。

而我现在，心细得就像一根断弦。
养得这么好，一定懂政治，
于是，植物的礼貌就有了宇宙的深意。

一抬头，我瞥见了给它浇水的人。
她不是园丁，不过看起来她有更好的方法，
知道如何把水浇到点子上。

稍一比较，多数人的背后都有无数的秘密。
而她的秘密不在她身后，在我和菊花之间，
没错，她的秘密永远在她的前面。

Golden Secret Series

When I lower my head, I see only these chrysanthemums,
golden guides, the little hands curve up and out, like the cirrus of mollusks.
A careless glance composes them into bright yellow petals.

And right now, I am being as careful as a broken string.
Raised this well, they surely understand politics,
and so, the civility of plants shows something profound about the universe.

When I lift my head, I glimpse the person who waters them.
She isn't a gardener, but it looks like she has even better methods,
and knows to water right where it matters.

Generally speaking, most people have countless secrets behind them.
But instead of behind her, her secrets are placed between me and the
chrysanthemums, that's right, her secrets will always be in front of her.

万古愁丛书

在那么多死亡中，你只爱必死。
其他的方式都不过是
把生活当成了一杆称。其实呢，
生活得越多，背叛也就越多。
稍一掂量，诗歌就是金钱——
这也是史蒂文斯用过的办法，
为着让语言的跳板变得更具弹性。
有弹性，该硬的东西才会触及活力。
围绕物质旋转，并不可怕，
它有助于心灵形成一种新的语速。
发胖之后，你害怕你的天赋
会从黑夜的汗腺溜走。
你想戒掉用淋漓左右灿烂，
但你戒不掉。你偏爱巧克力和啤酒，
但是，天赋咸一点会更好。
莴笋炒腊肉里有诗的起点。
小辣椒尖红，样子可爱得就像是
从另一个世界里递过来的一双双小鞋。
你猜想，无穷不喜欢左派。所以说，
干什么，都难免要过绝妙这一关。
不滋味，就好像雨很大，但床单是干的。
做爱一定要做到前后矛盾，
绝不给虚无留下一点机会。
没有人能探知你的底线。
心弦已断，虎头用线一提，像豆腐。
但是你说，我知道你在说什么。
我确实说过，我可不想过于迷信——
凡不可知的，我们就该沉默。
而你只勉强赞同诗应该比宇宙要积极一点。

6

Endless Worry Series

Among so much dying, you prefer an inevitable death.
Everything else is merely
a way of treating life like a scale. In fact,
the more one lives, the more one is betrayed.
Weigh this thought for a moment, that poetry is money—
this was the measure Wallace Stevens used
to add more spring to the springboard of language.
Only spring gives vigor to things that should be firm.
Revolving in a whirlpool of materiality isn't so bad,
it can help the spirit form a new quicker speech.
After you get fat, you fear your talent
will sweat away in the night.
You want to stop using fervor to master brilliance,
but you can't give it up. You prefer chocolate and beer,
though a saltier talent is better.
Stir-fried pork and asparagus is a starting point for poetry.
The tips of the hot peppers are red, as lovely as
tiny pairs of shoes brought from another world.
You suspect that the infinite doesn't like leftists. Therefore,
whatever you do, you have to go beyond the level of cleverness.
Flavorless as a hard rain, but the bed sheets are dry.
Always make love to the point of contradiction,
and never give nothingness an opportunity.
No one can find your bottom line.
Once the heartstrings are broken, a noble face is strung up, soft as tofu.
But you say, I know what you're saying.
I've said it before, I mustn't be overly superstitious—
about the unknown, we should keep quiet.
You grudgingly agree poetry should be more dynamic than the universe.

人不能低于沉默，诗不能低于
人中无人。从这里，心针指向现实，
一个圆出现了：凡残酷的，就不是本质。
而一个圆足以解决飘渺。
稍一滚动，丰满就变成了完满，
晃动的乳房也晃动眼前一亮。
一个圆，照看一张皮。像满月照看
大地和道德。从死亡中掉下的
一张皮，使我再次看清了你。
凡须面对的，不倾心就不可能。
而一旦倾心，万古愁便开始令深渊发痒。

People shouldn't be reduced to silence, poetry shouldn't be reduced
to a nobody in the crowd. From here, the heart's needle points to reality,
and a circle emerges: no brutality is intrinsic.
But a circle is enough to get rid of indistinctness.
With a bit of rolling, shapely becomes successful,
swaying breasts sway brightly before the eyes.
A circle, eyeing a stretch of skin. Like a full moon eyeing
the earth and ethics. Skin sloughed off
the dead lets me see you clearly again.
Everything that must be confronted will be adored.
But with adoration, endless worry prickles the abyss.

原创性愉悦丛书

在我们之间有一只鸟。
只要你一睁眼，它就在飞。
它让我们渐渐适应了我们之间的最佳距离。
它给所有的感觉都插上了一对翅膀。

当它飞向你时，时间只剩下一厘米。
我第一次想捉住我自己。
我想在你面前，捕捉到一个带翅膀的我。
我第一次感觉到奇妙从未背叛过真理。

在我和你我之间有一种东西
飞得比鸟还快。我想在你我面前
松开一个全新的角色。它所有的重量加起来
也不会超过一只鸟。它有漂亮的头，

你随时可以借来一用。它有长长的尾巴，
你不妨用它们来翘一翘宇宙的神经。
你奇怪，这么小的一只鸟身上，
竟然有全部的生活的影子。

Delight in Creativity Series

In between us is a bird.
If you open your eyes, he flies away.
He helps us slowly adapt to our optimal distance.
He sticks all of perception onto a pair of wings.

When he flies toward you, only a centimeter of time remains.
For the first time, I wanted to catch hold of myself.
I wanted to seize that winged self before your eyes.
For the first time, I felt like wonder has never betrayed truth.

Between me and you and I there is something
that flies faster than a bird. Before our eyes I wanted
to relax into a new role. Its whole weight together
wouldn't be more than a bird. It has a beautiful head,

you can borrow it anytime. It has a long tail,
and you might as well use those nerves they lift the universe with.
You're amazed that on such a tiny bird body
all of life is reflected.

夜鸟丛书

我梦见，我们在一起时一直是三个人。
你说，那另外一个其实是只鸟。

我叫你的名字时，那只鸟也一直叫。
你叫我的名字时，它仍在叫。

它的叫声，像一根缀着夜露的管子，
从黝黑的窗外伸了进来。

我们安静下来时，它的叫声依然持续不断。
它的叫声有确定的含义，只是里面没有一个名字。

它的叫声里包含着一种更大的呼唤。
以前，我以为那不可能存在于人的叫喊之外。

Night Bird Series

I dreamt each time we're together, three people are there.
You said, the other is a bird.

When I call your name, the bird is also calling.
When you call my name, he's still calling.

His voice is like a pipe collecting night dew,
extending in from the dark window.

When we're quiet, his calls continue.
The calls imply something, but don't name names.

His calls contain another vaster cry,
a kind I thought only exist in human screaming.

留得青山在丛书

深长的，绝不只是意味。
但在人和事之间，只有意味配得上深长。
我经常感到人不站我这一边，
我也经常感到，人经不住
事情的考验。人，往往会低估
事物的美丽。比如，说到深长，
一个人对另一个人意味着
太阳可以睡在单人床上。一小时，
就能改变历史。两小时，就能动摇真理，
三小时，甚至令永恒走神。而枕头上的凹痕，
像一座海底火山的芳邻。迷死你真逗，
好多环节全乱套了。比如，菜单
被当成节目单递了上来。清蒸，还是乱炖？
最深的驯服很容易让自我显得肤浅。
我确实有点饿了。哪怕只是补充几口樱桃呢。
心灵的小南瓜饼，可有秘诀？
我饿在人还有另外一种可能性里。
回过神来，月亮也可以是用盐和香料腌成的
一块令狮子们垂涎的皎洁的驴肉。

As Long As There Are Green Hills Series

The profound isn't just a kind of implication.
But between things and people, only implication can match the profound.
I often feel that others aren't on my side,
I also often feel that people can't bear
to undergo the trials of experience. People often underestimate
the beauty of objects. For example, speaking of the profound,
what one person implies to another person
is that the sun can sleep on a twin bed. An hour
can change history. Two hours can shake the truth,
three hours can make even eternity forgetful. The indentations in the pillow
are like a neighbor to a seafloor volcano. It's fun to confuse you,
muddling the many links. For example, a menu
is handed over like a playbill. Steamed or stewed?
The self seems shallow after a deep taming.
I really am a bit hungry, if only for the replenishment of a few cherries.
The small pumpkin cake of the heart—does it have the secret to success?
I'm hungry inside man's other possibilities.
Calming down, the moon can also be marinated in salt and spices
into a bright piece of donkey meat for the tigers to drool over.

悠悠的不一定都是往事丛书

你也许是尘土，但你现在不是。
你也许会归于尘土，但你现在要面对的是另一种真理。
你终究会是尘土，但我可以肯定你现在还不是尘土。

没摸清情况的话，小小的尘土
会是一个巨大的舞台。尘土里有他们的真理。
飞扬的尘土，像马蹄下的世界观。

除了真理，你还喜欢在尘土里看到什么？
凡真相，难免被手脚。假象还能假到哪里去？
想克服真理的人最终都变成了小蜥蜴。

没有人能例外。这是不是说，
在变成尘土之前，每个人都有可能从时间里赎回
一些原本只属于生命之花的秘密。

The Remote Isn't Necessarily in the Past Series

You're likely dust, but right now you're not.
You'll likely return to dust, but right now you're facing another kind of truth.
In the end you'll be dust, but I can confirm that right now you're not yet dust.

Sizing up the situation, the tiny particles of dust
are an enormous stage. Their truth is in the dust.
The rising dust is a worldview beneath horse's hooves.

Aside from truth, what else do you like to see in the dust?
Reality has trouble not getting tricked. How false can false appearances get?
In the end, those who want to conquer truth turn into tiny lizards.

No one's an exception. Isn't that to say,
before becoming dust, each person may ransom back from time
a few secrets whose originals belong to the flowers of life.

原始角色丛书

多年前，我的肉体将我错过。
这事情本不该发生，但事实上，
已重复过多次。我的肉体是我的奇迹，
但这听上去太高调。我当时的想法是，
奇迹会减弱自由，且很有可能，
奇迹是堕落的另一种形式。我的肉体，悬挂着，
像成熟的苹果，随时都会坠落。
你知道，如果碰巧砸到脑袋上，
世界也许会再次开窍。我侧卧在草地上，
周围布满了夏日昆虫的各种思想。
我喜欢任何有节奏的事情。
草地上，不须提炼，昆虫的思想就很有节奏。
顺着那节奏，我似乎能摸到命运的把柄。
我带去了半瓶葡萄酒，嚼在嘴里的牛肉干
散发着牦牛的气息。我消磨着
仿佛再不会被错过的我。我的肉体
曾是三只刚刚爬过垭口的牦牛。
那里，阿坝的雪水像透明的琴弦，
曾溶化过花岗岩比还坚硬的记忆。
我的肉体将我错过，意思是，从一开始，
我的肉体就由属于一个男人的肉体
和属于一个复活者的肉体组成。
它们带给我的快乐像真理一样矛盾。
但是，盲目的，从来就不是肉体，
你知道，我能解释的，还远不止这些。

The Original Role Series

Many years ago, my body passed me by.
It shouldn't have happened, but in fact,
it's happened many times. My body is my miracle,
but that sounds too grandiose. At the time I thought
miracles would weaken freedom, and it's likely
miracles are another form of degeneration. My body, hanging
like a ripe apple, could fall at any moment.
You know, if it happens to fall on a head,
the world might be set straight again. I lie in the grass,
with the summer insects' many thoughts around me.
I like anything with rhythm.
No need to refine anything in the grass, the insects' thoughts have rhythm.
In that rhythm, I seem to be able to touch the reins of fate.
I brought half a bottle of wine, chewing jerky
and breathing out yak breath. I'm wearing down
the self that likely won't be passed by again. My body
was once three yaks summiting a mountain pass.
There, Aba's snow was like a transparent piano string
that once melted memories more solid than granite.
My body has passed me by, which means, from the beginning
my body has belonged to a man's body
and a resurrected body conjoined.
The happiness that both have brought is as conflicted as the truth.
But, what is blind has never been my body—
You know, I have explanations for far more than this.

人在台北丛书

在北京和台北之间有一首诗，
因人而不异。一个明显的例子就是
诗里有能刺激我的"泥土的分寸"。
我在北京生活，时间总能从时间中多出来。

我在台北反生活，时间太短了，露出了
时间的狐狸尾巴。时间太短了，
说明下一次还有更好的机会。
或者，在北京和台北之间有一种湿，

但因人而异。激发我的是
湿里有"太阳的事业"。这令我猛然想起
诗的暧昧。伟大啊。直觉不直觉的，
反倒小意思了。你理解了湿，

自然也就理解了诗。我在台北原想讨论
诗是一种慢。一个简单的例子就是
湿也是一种慢。姜涛听后跃跃欲试，
发誓要对着干：诗也可以是一种快。

没错，姜母鸭的姜，滋味全在于奥秘。
稍一提示，时间的翅膀便含在了口中。
有没有根本性的遭遇呢？细雨里有喜雨，
从夜市回来，我迈出了雨人的脚步。

In Taipei Series

Between Beijing and Taipei is a poem,
and so to each his own. One clear example is
the stimulating line: "the earth's restraint."
Living in Beijing, I gain more time out of time.

Living in Taipei, time was too short, it revealed
time's tricky foxtail. Time was too short,
meaning next time will be even better.
Or, between Beijing and Taipei is a kind of dampness,

but it's different for everyone. What stimulates me is
that in the dampness is the "business of the sun." This makes me think
suddenly of poetry's ambiguity. How powerful! Intuitive or not,
it's actually of little importance. You understand dampness,

just as nature understands poetry. In Taipei I wanted to say
that poetry is a kind of slowness. A simple example is
dampness is also a kind of slowness. Hearing this and wanting to have a go,
the poet Ginger Tao vowed to do the opposite: poetry is also a kind of speed.

It's true, the ginger flavor in ginger duck is a mystery.
Let me point out, the wings of time are held in the mouth.
Are there essential encounters? From the drizzle comes a seasonal rain,
on the way back from the night market, I match the strides of a man in rain.

人在花莲丛书

小地方有大味道，除了温州馄饨的味道
还有莲雾的味道，除了野水仙的味道
还有大海的味道，除了释迦麻薯饼的味道
还有鳗鱼的味道，除了空气很新鲜
还有说不出的自然的新鲜。我得出的结论是
人尽可以矛盾于生活，但不该
矛盾于花开花落。人之花
艰难于人之树，但这从来就不是

一个很好的理由。早上醒来，
太阳像一个金钩子，钓我们身上的鱼。
没上钩，是运气；不上钩，是真的很好玩。
但好玩，顶多是表明底线不复杂。
很明显，大海在此有两个意思——
轰鸣的巨浪像蓝熨斗，试图将我们的经验抚平。
而我们身体里的大海，纯度突然增高，
将我们的个性掀翻在鸢尾花的码头。

外地人的眼光只是一种投影，
投射得越多，受骗的机会就会越小。
讲感情，命运吊诡于本能里
有一个深入浅出的你。论归宿，
人生大可平凡于天赋很重要，但绝对没有
你想象得那么重要。本地的屏幕上，
只有蔚蓝的风俗始终保持连贯。
每一秒钟，自我都取之不尽。

In Hualien Series

A small place of vast smells—along with the smell of Wenzhou wontons
is the smell of wax apples, along with the smell of wild narcissus
is the smell of the ocean, along with the custard-apple mochi
is the smell of eel, and along with the fresh air
is the ineffable freshness of nature. I conclude
that man can be conflicted by life, but shouldn't
be conflicted by the lifecycle of flowers. People's flowers
suffer from people's trees, but that's never been

a compelling reason. Waking up in the morning,
the sun is like a golden hook, catching the fish of our bodies.
Not getting hooked is just luck; not taking the bait is fun.
But fun at best only demonstrates that our bottom line isn't complex.
It's clear that the ocean means two things here—
thundering waves are like a blue iron trying to smooth out our experiences.
While the ocean in our bodies, its purity suddenly heightened,
tosses our individuality onto an iris's wharf.

The vision of outsiders is only a projection,
the more they project, the less they'll be cheated.
Speaking of emotions, the paradox of fate comes from instinct
around a simply explained you. As for returning home,
it's important that life have a talent for ordinariness, but it isn't
as important as you think. On local screens,
only sky-blue traditions maintain their connections.
At any moment, the self is inexhaustible.

恢复到天机不可泄露，还是没见底。
我由此想到，真正的恢复，应该是
专门针对男人的秘密而设置的一个主题。
说起来，风光似乎有限一点会更好。
本地的风光将时间的真理淘汰在
太平洋的边上。用手随便一指，
蓝天就比白天大。我能发现的秘密确乎是
在花莲，白天很大，夜晚很小。

To recover nature's mysteries means we haven't seen through it.
So I think, a real recovery should be
a theme configured to directly address men's secrets.
Speaking of which, it would be better if the scenery were limited.
The local scenery takes the truth of time and relegates it
to the banks of the Pacific. Pointing with any finger,
the blue sky is bigger than the day. The secret I can discover is surely
that in Hualien, the days are vast and the nights are quite small.

对手戏丛书

这游戏到份上，只好听从桂花的安排了。
小河边，桂花将飘香的骰子掷进生活，
它赌你能听见远方的心跳。
这世上只有两种人：一种是喜爱桂花的人，
一种是对桂花毫无感觉的人。

小黄花瓣制作美酒的小分币——
不用找钱了。永恒一泡就软，可口如浪尖上
有一个只有你才能跳得最好的舞。
你赞成这样的区分，因为这些桂花
比我们所能想象得更忠实于生活。

美妙时，人生经不起一吸——
没有界限，不需要准备太多的东西。
不就是起伏比平常更明显吗。
不就是体验比深刻更本质吗。
不就是暗香比禁忌更刺激吗。

用美妙的底气，你把我吸进肺里。
太深了，就好像有一个宇宙
只为桂花香而存在。换气时，
有一个秘密稀释了虚无；从此以后，
没有人知道我会变成怎样的对手。

Matched Players Series

The game has gone this far, let the osmanthus flowers plan the rest.
By the riverbank, osmanthus casts the dice of fragrance into life,
it bets you can hear a faraway heartbeat.
This world has only two types of people: those who love osmanthus,
and those who feel nothing for it.

The little yellow petals create small coins of liquor—
no need to make change. Soaked they get soft, delicious as the tip of a wave
that can only dance its best when you're there.
You agree with such distinctions, because these osmanthus flowers
are more faithful to life than we can imagine.

In moments of wonder, a human life can't bear to inhale—
there are no boundaries, there's no need to prepare so much.
Isn't tumult clearer than ordinariness?
Isn't life experience more intrinsic than profundity?
Isn't a faint lingering fragrance more exciting than abstinence?

With wondrous stamina, you breathe me into your lungs.
So deep it seems there is a universe
that only exists for the fragrance of osmanthus. Breathing out,
a secret dilutes the nothingness; from now on,
no one knows what kind of match I'll become.

生活的艺术丛书

从生活中醒来，我得到了一块冰。
它严肃而阴冷，比最矛盾的礼物还要坚硬。
它反射出的光里有十只鸭子的胃口。

鲜明的棱角滴下的水珠
像最小的命运，因不断重复自我
而听上去像一种透明的音乐——

它的大小和马戏团用的兽笼差不多。
如果把它推向一头狮子，需要很多工具。
我可不想让千斤顶也掺和进来。

我现在只想回到一种简单的立场。
我不需要做太多的移动。
我将这冰块立起来，竖在爱情的对面。

我猜想生活的艺术就是这么诞生的：
随着时间的流逝，巨大的冰块会不断融合。
汩汩的融水会因四处流淌，渗到地下，并获得

一种象征的力量。我也可以将冰块竖立在
让你感到困惑的任何事物的对面；不过那样的话，
你得先告诉我，你是否喜欢冰的真理。

The Art of Life Series

Waking up in the middle of life, I receive a piece of ice.
It is solemn and cold, harder than the most ambivalent gift.
The light it reflects back has the appetite of ten ducks.

The droplets that drip from its bright corners
are like the smallest destinies, repeating themselves endlessly
to sound like some sort of transparent music—

It's about the size of a circus cage.
To push it toward a lion would take many tools.
I wouldn't think of letting a hoisting jack mess with it.

Right now I just want to return to a simple position.
I don't need to move too much.
I'll put this piece of ice on its end, across from love.

I'm guessing the art of life is born of this:
with the passage of time, enormous chunks of ice will continue to melt.
The water will gurgle in all directions, seep into the earth, and garner

a symbolic power. I could also stand the ice upright
across from any one of the things that puzzle you; but for that,
you'd have to tell me whether you like the truths the ice tells.

假如种子不死丛书

我的工作对象有很多，
我的服务对象却少而又少。
我用白云工作，用冰山工作，用彩虹工作，
原材料越大，空间就越刺激。

我用新月加班到黑暗的心脏。
但我只服务于诗，将语词和种子并列在一起。
我使用镜子像使用筛子，
习惯了，自然就会有窍门。

我信任镜子里的光，也喜欢筛子上的小眼睛。
我会使劲摇晃。没跳过舞的种子
不是好种子。我可不想错过好种子。
我会用心筛选的。剧烈的颤动

对每个人都是一次启发。
动静太大了，想不天真已来不及了。
想天真，只能面对一种后果：
天是用来晕眩的，地是用来摇滚的。

我才不在乎我的服务对象晃起来时
样子好看不好看呢。我在乎的是雨下得大不大。
我会给每个词都挖上一个小坑，
一个种子也想跳下去的小坑。

Imagine Seeds Never Die Series

I have so much to work on,
and so little to serve.
I use the clouds to work, and icebergs, and rainbows,
the bigger the raw material, the more exciting the space.

With the new moon, I work late into a dark heart.
But I serve only poetry, juxtaposing words and seeds.
I use a mirror like a sieve,
and along with practice come the tricks of the trade.

I trust the light in mirrors, and I like the sieve's small eyes.
I'll shake it as hard as I can. Seeds that have never danced
aren't the good seeds. I don't want to miss the good seeds,
I'll sieve them out carefully. A violent shaking

can inspire anyone.
Too much motion, and it's too late to lose innocence.
If one wants to be innocent, one can only face the consequences:
the sky is there for vertigo, the earth is there to quake.

When what I serve begins to shake I don't care
if it looks good or not. I care whether the rain is heavy.
I'll dig a little hole for each word,
the kind of hole a seed would want to leap into.

两个男孩中的一个
已死于破碎的记忆。但可怕的
不是已破碎的。要么就是三个男孩中的一个
已死于毒奶粉。但最可怕的
不是有毒。假如是你，你还敢信任
没有破碎过的心吗？没有破碎过的心
是一封绑在鹤腿上的信。它比飞翔还要原始，
它不开窍，但并不天真。意思就是，
它绝不会在你开窍之前被意外打开。
你会躺在这首诗的左边读到它的。
你将有两次和左边有关的机会，
这就好像真正的天真
不在没有破碎过的事物中。
假定你从未见过那男孩，在仅次于微妙的事物里，
你会如何排列你我的心花？
宇宙的心花还经得起一问吗？
你还敢信任心花吗？当它微妙到非人的怒放。
或者，当它再次回到原型，破碎的镜子
已被打扫到簸箕里。你肯定拿过扫帚，
干过这样的事情。这用不着太多的假设。

The Heart of China Series

Of two boys one
is dead in broken memory. But the horror
hasn't broken. Or it's three boys among whom one
has died of poisoned milk powder. But the horror of it
isn't the poison. If it were you, would you still dare believe
in a heart that hasn't been broken? An unbroken heart
is a letter tied to the leg of a crane. More primal than flying,
it never matures, though it isn't innocent. That is to say,
it would never accidentally unfold before you begin to mature.
You'll read it as you lie on the left side of this poem.
You'll have your two chances with the right side,
and it seems true innocence
isn't to be found in broken things.
Suppose you'd never seen that boy in those nearly subtle objects,
how would you arrange our happy hearts?
Can the happy heart of the universe still endure the question?
Do you still dare to trust a happy heart? Even when it's so subtle
        as to break into inhumane bloom.
Or, when it returns again to prototype, the broken mirror
has been swept into a dustpan. Of course you've used a broom before
to do that sort of thing. That much we can assume.

牵线人丛书

看什么，都必须先要转过脸去，
这就是她。假如是直接面对，
她会比地震中的一条狗还要紧张。
怎么看世界，都不如一只猫那样顺眼。

她有时会控制不住在人狗间有一种比较。
她对待猫比对待狗更严肃。
她曾说服自己要像爱猫一样爱上一个人。
她的结论是，爱怎么比数学还难。

她苦于灵魂不愿被束缚，
与她为敌的事物里，有大学，地铁和电视。
电视里的野兽会从屏幕里跑出来，舔她的眉毛和耳环。
这样的事，好像不止发生过好几回。

于是，每一样需要接触的东西
最终都变成了一种需要克服的事情。
她对环境有特殊的敏感。她不断地换环境——
在一个地方呆太久了，人就会变成废墟。

于是，她比任何人都更频繁地从废墟中走出来。
这似乎是她的不可抗拒的规律。
她自己偶尔也能认识到这一点。
新欢中已有无人能意识到的瑕疵，

她受不了瑕疵。或者说，她受不了
别人也会有她身上的那些瑕疵。
不完全是需要缓和矛盾的问题，
记忆里，旧爱在飘渺中似乎稍好一点。

The Go-Between Series

To look, you have to turn your head—
that's her. If you face her directly,
she'll be edgier than a dog in an earthquake.
However you see the world, nothing's easier to look at than a cat.

Sometimes she can't help but compare people and dogs.
She takes cats even more seriously.
She once convinced herself she should love a person like she loves cats.
Her conclusion: how can love be harder than math?

She suffers because her soul won't be fettered,
and among her enemies is the university, the subway, the TV.
Wild animals on TV burst from the screen to lick her eyebrows and earrings.
It seems that's happened many times.

And so, everything that requires contact
becomes something that must be dealt with.
She has a special sensitivity to her environment. She keeps switching—
if she stays too long in one place, she's ruined.

So she walks out of ruins more often than anyone.
It seems to be an irresistible pattern.
Sometimes she can recognize that herself.
In a new lover there is always an imperceptible flaw,

and she can't stand flaws. Or you could say, she can't stand
that others might have her same flaws.
It's not entirely a question of mitigating contradictions,
in her memory, old loves linger and seem slightly better.

洗脑算什么。腰被洗了，
才是被洗彻底了。她知道这个世界上
存在着用腰思考的人。下面垫得再高点，
她也许会在最遥远的地方看见这首诗的尾巴。

What's the big deal about brainwashing? Only when we wash our loins
are we truly clean. She knows that on this earth
there are people who think with their loins. Raise her up a bit,
and perhaps she'll see the tail of this poem from afar.

思想轨迹丛书

你有思想，它不同于人们曾告诉你的
各种结局：不论那是生命的结局，
还是宇宙的结局。你有思想的火花，
它不同于人们能看到的各种情形。
哦，火花。轮子的转动
溅起了肉体的崇高。你有思想，
所以你不可能把肉体想象成
别的事情。你有思想的对象，
它不同于现实的对立面。哦，对象，
它黑暗于光明对黑暗的无知。
你有思想，它不同于人们所熟悉的
深入或者复杂；是的，它不同于
人们所曾有过的无尽的悲哀，或惨痛的损失。
你有灵活的思想，它不同于阴郁的人
对新诗所寄予的渴望。没错，它不同于
那些无理的深渊，或是浅薄的呼吁。
你有思想，它不同于人们
在暴力和命运之间做出的选择，
它不会简单于神话里没有血。
你有火红的思想，它不同于城市的风景，
也不同于人们对荒野的态度。
不是你不天真，而是你不会把荒野
看成是另外的事物。不是你的记忆
不够强大，而是你和诗的关系更微妙。
哦，微妙。你有思想，它不同于
人常常被人性毁灭，也不同于野兽
从不得益于兽性。你不需要具体的例子，
哦，有太多这样的例子了。你的罕见的耐心

Orbit of a Thought Series

You have a thought, and it's different from the endings
others have told you about, whether it's the end of life
or the end of the universe. You have the spark of a thought,
and it's different from the situations people can perceive.
Ah, sparks. The revolutions of the wheel
splatter the body's sublimity. You have a thought,
so you cannot imagine the body
as some other thing. Your thought has an object,
and it's different from reality's antithesis. Ah, the object
is dark from the ignorance light has of darkness.
You have a thought, and it's different from what people know
of depth and complexity. Yes, it's different
from the endless grief and losses people have had.
You have flexible thoughts, different from the hopes
pessimists place in new poetry. Yes, it's different
from those unreasonable abysses or shallow breaths.
You have a thought, and it's different from the choices
people make when caught between violence and fate,
it won't be as simple as a myth without blood.
You have a fiery thought, and it's different from the city scenery,
different from how people view the wilderness.
It isn't that you're not innocent, but that you won't see the wilderness
as some other thing. It isn't that your memory
isn't good enough, but that your connection to poetry is more subtle.
Ah, subtlety. You have a thought, and it's different from
how humans are destroyed by human nature, it's different from wild animals
never profiting from their animal nature. You don't need specific examples,
examples abound. Your uncommon patience

不会针对你的形象。凡已损失的，
未必不是被筛选掉的。哦，形象，
你有强大的思想，诗才会超越你我，
变成没有比诗更现实的东西。

won't be directed towards your image. All that has been lost
hasn't necessarily been sifted away. Ah, the image—
only when you have a profound thought will poetry surpass you and me,
and there will be nothing more real than a poem.

百日红丛书

观赏性很强，但种植却从不普遍，
这就是你的命运。你的歌
是野鸽子的彩虹。我入迷得很晚，
但是毫无保留。对此，我感到十分骄傲。
我入迷，并且一旦入迷，就好像爱
已不足以构成一次跨越。
我想在最短的时间里缩短
我们之间的距离。为什么见到你之前，
我没想过我可以用这样的方式
抓紧我自己？我入迷，翘尾巴回敬
各种花样翻新的寂寞宇宙。
并且一旦入迷，我不记得还有什么东西是
比我们正使用着的语言更宽的鸿沟。
我开始有被羽毛爱上的感觉。
我想我会找到一种办法，把你给予我的友谊
再带回给你。我知道你从未听到过
斧子的声音。你并不因此而脆弱。
无论那些蠢货们对你说过什么，
我都愿意替他们向你道歉。
我单膝跪地，但愿藏在你背后的精灵们
能看见我。因为有时候，我更愿使用
清晰的姿态而不是绽放的语言。

Crape Myrtle Series

Lovely to look at, but not often grown,
that is your fate. Your song
is a rainbow of wild pigeons. I was enchanted late
but then held nothing back. I'm proud of that.
I was enchanted, and right away it was as though love
wasn't enough of a leap.
I wanted to shrink the distance between us
as quickly as possible. Why is it that before I saw you
I never thought I could
take hold of myself this way? I was enchanted, cockily complimenting
the lonely, ever-changing universe.
As soon as I was enchanted, I remembered other things
that are greater chasms than the languages we use.
I began to feel I was loved by feathers.
I think I'll find a way to take the friendship you've given me
and return it to you. I know you've never heard
the sound of the axe. But that doesn't mean you're weak.
No matter what those idiots have said to you,
I apologize for them.
I'll get down on one knee, hoping the spirits behind you
can see me. Because sometimes I'd rather use
a clear gesture than flowery language.

都是谜丛书

你们周围的一切，你们之中的一切，都是谜
——伏尔泰

一个陌生的女人保佑着他
——里尔克

生活就是星空。假如你需要，
我愿意转让下一个命名权。
请把头稍抬起一点，请从这个角度再确定一次。
假如你只是不解，我愿意再重复一遍
我们的天真之歌。每一种黑暗
都很空洞。心，兀自将宇宙的孤独燃烧，
但发光的却是钻石。巨大的，坚硬的，
经过加工的钻石，向四周投射出
生命的反光。场景很原始，就好像它是
为野人准备的，而你，
不过是发现了诗歌之谜的几种用途。

这里，西红柿种子不论斤卖，
五块钱一小袋。不还价，不甜不要钱。
而要买到小黄瓜的种子，你必须打赌。
没想到苦瓜的种子外形会这么漂亮，
像天赋一样饱满。记住，最深邃的友谊
是由种子带来的。南边，是嘈杂的工地
和热闹的农贸市场。北边是废弃的纺织厂，
东边，按午间新闻里的说法，民办小学
顽强地构筑了底层的真相。西边，
浑圆的落日照常给生活的边缘
带去了一枚火红的纪念章。根据心理史，

Everything Is Riddles Series

Everything around and between you is a riddle.
—Voltaire

An unfamiliar woman blessed him.
—Rilke

Life is a starlit sky. If you needed it,
I'd give you naming rights.
Tilt your head up, and reconfirm from that angle.
If it's just that you don't understand, I'll repeat
our songs of innocence. Every type of darkness
is a void. Only the heart burns up the loneliness of the universe,
but what gives out light is diamonds. Enormous, hard,
processed diamonds reflect the light
of life everywhere. The scene is primeval, as though it were
set up for primitive men, but you've merely
discovered a few uses for poetry's riddles.

Here, tomato seeds aren't sold by the pound,
but for five yuan per small bag. No bargaining, refunds if they're not sweet.
But if you want to buy cucumber seeds, you have to make a wager.
I never thought bittermelon seeds would be so pretty,
plump as talent. Remember, the deepest friendships
are brought by seeds. To the south is a noisy construction site
and a bustling farmer's market. To the north is an abandoned textile mill,
to the east, according to the midday news, an independent elementary school
stubbornly builds the reality of the bottom rungs. To the west,
as usual, the circular setting sun pins to the edge of life
a fiery badge. According to psychology,

每一种安慰，都是深刻的妥协；
否则，你得到的，就是十足的赝品。
美丽的面孔，几个女人因你而具体，
具体到大海也会枯干。她们纷纷来到海边，
为受伤的记忆献出她们手提包里的
各种小物件。润肤膏，创可贴，避孕套，
口红，长命锁。你被打开过几次？或者，
从什么时候开始，你不再为恸哭而流泪？
你是否愿意在细雨和拯救之间
建立起某种联系？细雨已经落下，
盘山公路上，陌生的女人，你仍是我的一切。

every kind of comfort is a compromise;
otherwise everything you get is counterfeit.
With their beautiful faces, a few women become concrete because of you,
so concrete the oceans will dry up. They come one by one to the shore,
and donate little objects from their handbags
to a painful memory. Moisturizer, band-aids, condoms,
lipstick, protective charms. How many times have you opened up? Or,
when did it start, and when will you stop crying over your pain?
Are you hoping to create a link
between the fine rain and rescue? A fine rain is falling
along the winding mountain road, and you, unfamiliar women,
          you're still my everything.

反宇宙体验丛书

半山腰间，短暂的幸福
轻飘如云雾。万刃山迎头赶上
一只山隼定下的调门。它出现了七次。
它的完美的盘旋，一次比一次
接近对人生的回敬。那确乎是
一个起点，在半空中，它就开始捕捉
最佳的时机。它不挑剔目标，
不在乎田鼠或野兔是否配得上
它的突击行动。一旦最佳的角度确定，
它就开始冲刺，给死亡带去
一个绝对的速度。表演重复了无数次，
但没有一个猎物知道如何称呼
这种结局。而短暂的幸福矛盾于
只有我们才知道如何定义结局。
半山腰间，云雾和天籁组成了
新的序曲。在1997和1998年之间，
还剩下多少时间？三个谈论新茶和草药的人中
有我的脱颖而出。我先是接受了
蜜蜂的请求，允许它们按摩
我的化身。接着，我顺从了蝴蝶的逻辑，
从生命的失败中微妙只有我知道
你的骄傲曾有多么重要。

An Anti-Universe Experience Series

Halfway up the mountain, a brief happiness
floats in like mist. Mt. Wanren tries to catch up
to the mountain falcon's pitch. He appears seven times.
His perfect spirals come closer and closer
to a response to life. That is indeed
a starting point, and in midair, he starts to seize
the most opportune moments. He isn't picky about his goal,
doesn't care if the field mouse or hare is worthy
of his surprise attack. As soon as he determines the optimum angle,
he begins to dive, giving death
an absolute velocity. The performance is repeated countless times,
but none of his prey knows what to call
the ending. This temporary happiness conflicts
with the fact that only I know how to define this ending.
Halfway up the mountain, the mist and the sounds of nature combine
into a new overture. How much time remains
before 1997 turns to 1998? Among the three of us discussing tea and
Chinese medicine
I come to the fore. First I accept
the entreaties of honeybees, and let them massage
my current incarnation. Then, following the logic of butterflies,
in the subtle failures of life, only I know
how important your pride once was.

金银花丛书

几只野猫从它们的领地里
警惕地，盯住从竹林后面走出的
一伙人：在它们和我们之间，
距离的每一次微妙的改变，
都意味着动物很政治。

没错，在它们玻璃子弹般的眼睛里，
有一个不为我们所知的世界。
但是，你不必道歉。你不必担心
剩下的谜本来就已经很少。你也不必解释
谜，从来就拒绝有自己的风格。

现在，向五月的风格提供例子的
是这几株茂盛的金银花。现实中的火
越抽象，它们的药用价值就越高；
尽管被喷过防虫剂，但加工它们的过程
仍是朴素的。你不会声称你从未采摘过东西吧。

Honeysuckle Series

From their territory, a few feral cats
watch warily as from behind a bamboo grove
a gang of men emerge: between us and them,
every tiny adjustment of distance
demonstrates just how political animals are.

Indeed, in their glass bullet eyes
is a world unknown to us.
But don't apologize. No need to worry.
Very few riddles remain. You don't need to explain
that riddles have always refused their own style.

Now, what offers an example of May's style
are these flourishing honeysuckle trees. The more abstract
the fire of reality, the more it's worth as medicine.
Even sprayed with pesticides, its processing
is still pure. Tell me you wouldn't claim you've never picked anything.

端午节丛书

如果让我去比较这两个世界——
一个是有你在里面包粽子的世界,
一个是门上插着菖蒲的有待进一步解释的世界。

被碧绿的楝树叶包起来的感觉真好,
其次才是这些洞庭湖出产的糯米
静静地浸泡在温柔的陶器中。

其次才是你说馅里必须有红枣,
以及必不可少的花样就是,滑动的龙舟
取代了火车头,朝着镜中飞奔而去。

Dragon Boat Festival Series

If you ask me to compare these two worlds—
one is a world with you making sticky-rice dumplings,
one is a world with a door of calamus awaiting further explanation.

The greened chinaberry leaves fold nicely around the dumplings,
and then there is this sticky-rice grown by Dongting Lake
soaking quietly in a warm earthenware pot.

And then there is you saying the filling must have jujubes,
it mustn't lack variety, and the sliding dragon boats
replace the trains, speeding into the mirror.

从舷窗上俯瞰下去，灯火像发亮的海藻
漂浮在黑暗的潮水中。广大的灯火
正慢慢加热你以为再也看不到的东西。
巨变难移沧桑。心灵的代价
怎么就不朴素了呢。本性从来就可耻，
但是天性就不一样了，可以琢磨的地方有很多。
这里拧拧，那里还应再紧紧。
精神的螺丝钉可是比精神更幽默，
你最好能早点波及到这一点。
没错，久违的温暖也许还不能说明什么问题，
而人间的黑暗就在这样的高度之下。

New Observation Series

Looking down through the porthole, lights float like glistening kelp
in dark tidal waters. The broad lights
slowly warm things you thought you'd never see again.
External changes can't touch inner experience. How can the price a soul pays
not be simple? Our traits have always been disgraceful,
but our nature is not, and there are many ways to improve.
Pinched and prodded here, tucked and tidied there.
The screws of consciousness are more amusing than consciousness itself,
it's best to involve that as soon as you can.
A long-awaited warmth likely can't illustrate the issue,
but life's darkness is there below this height.

宇宙的寂寞已不在话下。
但这样的雄浑太具体，并不适合每个人。
你开放，将缠绵带到地上，但你不知道他们
在你的开放中看到的究竟是什么。
人和人之间的不同曾让你手里握着的种子紧张。
也许，那距离并不可耻，但要缩短它，
却怎么都不可能。无辜已试过人性，爱也已试过
大自然的神奇。而那距离仍然没有消除。
你开放，在关键之处，将我重新编织到
花的神圣中。一转身就化身，怎么办？
你比我想得更多的是你真的和生命结合过吗？
其次才是新角色中的旧情绪。
风里来，悠悠同样很矛盾；白云的名字里
有你喜欢的大雁的踪影。人字会飞，才不在乎南北呢。
雨里去，浩淼同样不渺小很孤独。
你的泪水是彩虹的绷带。
那被缠过的东西，有很多次，虚无到了极点，
却在诗生活中深深地扎下根。

The Roots of Wisdom Series

The loneliness of the universe goes without saying.
But such insistence is too specific, it doesn't go for everyone.
You open up and bring tenderness to the earth, but you don't know
what others see in your openness.
People's differences once made the seeds in your hand nervous.
Perhaps that distance isn't shameful, but there's no way
to shorten it. Innocence has tested human nature, and love has tested
the magic of nature. Yet that distance hasn't been dispelled.
You open up beyond the hinges and weave me anew
into the holiness of flowers. Turn around and it's a new life, what's there to do?
Do you think more than I do about whether you've integrated into life?
Only then is there a new role for old emotions.
The wind arrives, and its casualness is conflicted; in the name of white clouds
are traces of those wild geese you like. People's words fly, with no
       concern for direction.
The rain departs, and the vastness is lonely not paltry.
Your tears are rainbowed bandages.
These tangled things are again and again the apex of emptiness,
but they still plant their roots deep in a life of poetry.

尼罗河白莲丛书

最初，你叫不出它们的名字。
但是，第一眼，这些犹如伸出的蓝色拳头的非洲白莲
便在你的心里获得了一个位置。
一个位置，就像章鱼的吸盘一样有力，
许多生活的意义不停地向它游去。
被吸进去，被那些仿佛与我们的消化器官很相像的
内在构造奇妙成一叠记忆的小夹子。
再夹紧些，就好像这是把事情清理干净的第一步。
以前没怎么用过，不是你的错。
它们夹住的东西或许可叫做宇宙的彩色活页。
没想象得那么重，很好翻；
也很好玩，有点像重温翻身的隐喻史。
解放啰。动一下，就是虚无已死。
解脱啰！我们的身体其实和这些石蒜科植物一样，
并不讨厌朴素的逻辑。变种有很多，动不动，就绰约。
突出的特点是，绿叶的形状像裸体的剑。
是的，任何时候，不要轻易就说我们一无所有。
沿着它们的秘密旅途，从未得到过的奖赏
开始有了新的原型。很多时候，性无疑比爱更美妙，
但赢得我们的心灵的，是孤独的爱。

White Lotuses on the Nile Series

At first you didn't know what to call them.
But with one glance, these African white lotuses with thrusting blue fists
won a place in your heart.
It's a place with the draw of an octopus' sucker,
much of life's significance keeps moving toward it.
Drawn in, and by an innate intestine-like structure,
somehow turned into pincers of memory.
Pinching tighter, this seems to be the first step toward tidying up.
It's not your fault you've never used them before.
What they grab onto might be called the universe's colorful loose-leaf binder.
It isn't as heavy as one might think, easy to flip through.
Funny, it's a little like a metaphorical history of resuscitation.
Released. Move about, the nothingness is dead.
Free at last! Our bodies are like these lycoris plants,
they're not bothered by simple logic. Many varieties, all effortlessly graceful.
Their prominent trait is that their leaves are shaped like naked swords.
Yes, don't ever rashly proclaim that we have nothing.
Along their secret journey, unreceived rewards
begin with a new prototype. Sex is often better than love,
but lonesome love is what wins over our souls.

向命运致敬丛书

……，不，激发我兴趣的是"神性"。
——艾马纽尔·列维纳斯

你听见有人喊，维拉，快跑。
转身望去，你看见一个手里抱着花布包的女人
长发翻飞，在对面的街道上
快速地奔跑着。你在电影里见过

拼命追赶移动的火车的女人——
没有眼泪，奔跑结束时，就好像
命运被狠狠踩了一下。你熟悉
那贯注的表情，那从额头流下的

大如玉米粒的汗珠。你没追赶过火车
既不说明你很幸运，也不说明你就有缺憾；
只说明你有过的爱情和开走的火车无关。
你也许还不太了解那机械性的蛮力

能从我们的身体中带走些什么。
大街上，人流如落叶，物质的无辜
长过了王菲唱一首老歌所需要的时间。
你并不认识这奔跑的女人，不过，

几乎所有认识和不认识她的人都在喊——
维拉，快跑。你能感到她的速度越来越快，
快得像从现实的死角里拔出的一根刺。
很可能，有过一个瞬间，她甚至跑得比命运还快。

Paying Respects to Fate Series

> ". . . No, what interests me is 'spirituality.'"
> —Emmanuel Lévinas

You hear someone shout, Lola, run!
Spinning around, you see a woman clutching a cloth purse
her long hair flying, dashing
down the opposite sidewalk. You've seen in the movies

a woman sprinting for a train—
no tears, though when the race ends, it seems
fate has been cruelly trampled. You know
that look of concentration, that forehead dripping

with beads of sweat like corn kernels. That you've never sprinted for a train
doesn't mean you're lucky, nor that you're flawed;
it only means the love you've felt and the trains you've taken are unrelated.
You likely don't know what sheer mechanical strength

can take from our bodies.
People stream over the street like falling leaves, and materiality's innocence
lasts longer than an old Wang Fei song.
You don't know the running woman, but

it seems those who know her and those who don't are all shouting—
Lola, run! You can feel her going faster and faster,
as fast as a thorn being extracted from a blind spot of reality.
Soon she might run faster than fate.

太快了。一个又一个金黄的桔子,
开始从她紧抱着的花布包里散落出来。
你从地上拣起桔子,也开始奔跑起来。
别担心,这首诗里会有一个终点的。

Too fast. One after another, golden tangerines
begin to drop from her cloth purse.
You pick them up and start to run. . . .
No, no need to worry—this poem will come to an end.

假如没有笼子丛书

他有自己的角度，从这个角度看去，
他对世界做出的选择远远多于
世界对他做出的选择。你想看特别的收藏品
还是想看特殊的证据？你想知道
你对世界的选择有什么特别的地方吗？
世界是一块空地，美妙于他的选择。
而从他的角度看去，你并没有落后多少。

他选择收集笼子，各种各样的笼子
代表了形形色色的机遇。他为笼子编写的目录
看上去像布雷地图。他的俏皮话是
他还从未让一个笼子漏网过。笼子的背后
比笼子里面藏有更多的秘密。这也许是事实，
但却不是事情的全部。多少次，不管有没人在场，
他坚决不同意一切到笼子为止。

到笼子为止，其实就是到口号为止。
有时，笼子已经空了，他依然会站在笼子的对面，
伸直胳膊，指指点点；从这个角度看去，
他是这世上唯一和笼子真正争吵过的人。
也不妨说，他是笼子专家，软硬都有一套。
再抽象的笼子也逃不出笼子的命运。
比如，鸟笼里鸟人比鸟更逼真，

兽笼里除了有狮子还有美女。
而蛇的笼子是一场小品表演；有毒的，
往往比无毒的，更容易混淆在生命的美丽中。
比生命的美丽还吸引人的是，笼子拦不住最爱。

If There Were No Cages Series

He has his own perspective, and from that perspective,
the decisions he makes about the world far outnumber
the decisions the world makes about him. Do you want specific artifacts
or particular proof? Do you want to know
what's special about the decisions you make about the world?
The world is an empty space, more amazing than his decisions.
But from his perspective, you're not far behind.

He decides to collect cages, all sorts of different cages
representing many opportunities. He compiles a list of his cages
and it looks like a map of landmines. He wisecracks
that he's never let a cage slip through his net. There are more mysteries
hidden behind the cage than inside the cage. That's likely true,
but that isn't all. How many times, no matter how many people are there,
has he resolutely disagreed that everything ends with the cage?

Everything ends with the cage, in fact everything ends with a slogan.
Sometimes the cage is empty, and he'll stand in front of it,
gesticulating with his arms: from this perspective,
he's the only person on earth who's ever argued with a cage.
One might as well say, he's an expert in cages, using both carrot and stick.
Even an abstract cage can't escape a cage's fate.
For example, a birdbrain in a birdcage is more lifelike than a bird,

and a beast's cage will hold a woman along with a lion.
A snake's cage is a skit; the poisonous ones
get mixed up in the beauty of life more easily than the harmless ones.
What attracts people more than life's beauty is that cages can't hold back
the greatest love.

此外，你肯定不知道你曾在空气的笼子里
听到过最好听的歌。记住，到什么时候，
都是王菲的歌最好听。试试运气，

你也许会在声音的笼子里捕捉到两只蝴蝶。
从这个角度看去，蝴蝶的笼子
就是你不曾想象过花也会有笼子。
举例说吧，水仙花的笼子是最早把你比作水仙的陌生人。
你难道没有选择过让他感到陌生吗？
你收到过水仙花，所以，大地的笼子
尽管可怕，却从未输给过荒凉。

Moreover, you surely don't know that it was in a cage of air
that you once heard the loveliest song. Remember, at any moment,
Wang Fei's songs are the best. Try your luck,

and you might capture two butterflies in a cage of sound.
From that perspective, the butterflies' cage
is the cage you haven't yet imagined for flowers.
For example, the cage of narcissus flowers makes you feel like a stranger
            to the narcissus.
But haven't you made it feel like a stranger, too?
You've been given narcissus flowers before, and so, the cage of the earth
although terrible, has never lost out to desolation.

青烟丛书

年轻时你不会懂得爱与诗的
特殊关系。没有捷径可走，踉跄好比铿锵，
一旦养成习惯，觉悟会成就烙印；
而且事实上，曲折锻炼了美腿，
不长在你身上，更好看。
凡是好感，都难免要从你身上冒出一阵青烟。
辜负天赋是早晚的事。当然，
青烟也可以是尺子，就好像
风是运用尺子的大师。风力增大，
世界被吹来吹去。你心中的风暴
总会有一两人知道。但是年轻时你不会知道
什么是爱的艺术，也不会知道
诗有可能将友谊深入到那一步。
你甚至不会知道祝福你的力量有多么强大——
当你的父母反对你的时候，朝霞祝福你，
野葡萄祝福你。宇宙的幻觉也站在你一边。
虚度被再三提及，被上升到
云的高度。必要的虚度不止一点点。
虚度甚至设想过假如没有虚度的话，
你是否还值得信任。因为爱你虚度过我的诗，
因为诗你虚度我的爱。但是没关系，
长天的感觉真好，比例绝对没错，
古人的眼力没错；长天让野鹅的队形
看上去像一串飞翔的黑珍珠项链。
年轻时你不会想到有一天你会有勇气写到
年轻时你不懂诗的艺术包含了多少爱。

Green Mist Series

When you were young, you didn't understand the special connection
between love and poetry. There are no shortcuts, staggering is better
    than clattering,
and once that becomes a habit, realization will make its mark;
moreover, a beautiful torturously exercised leg
is prettier when it isn't part of your own body.
Any good feeling will end up oozing from your body in a green mist.
Failure to live up to talent is common. Of course,
a green mist can also be a measure, and it seems
the wind is a master of wielding measures. The wind picks up
and the world is blown around. Your heart's windstorms
will always be known to two people. But when you were young you didn't know
what the art of love is, and you didn't know
how deep poetry will take a friendship.
You didn't even know how powerful a blessing can be—
when your parents opposed you, the clouds of dawn blessed you,
the wild grape vines blessed you. The universe's illusions stood with you.
Time-wasting is mentioned over and over, it's lifted
to the clouds. But time-wasting is necessary, and not just a little.
Time-wasting has even wondered, if time-wasting didn't exist
would you be trustworthy? For love, you've wasted time on my poetry,
for poetry, you've wasted time on my love. But it doesn't matter,
the vast heavens are fine, the proportions are just right,
and our forefathers judged correctly; the heavens turn a formation of geese
into a necklace of flying black pearls.
When you were young, you never thought you'd be brave enough to write
that when you were young you had no idea poetry's art holds so much love.

人生角色丛书

男人和女人并排坐在栏杆上，
大海在下面，悬崖有三十米高——
越过他们的背影看去，海水蔚蓝，
颠簸着，在蔚蓝的颠簸中，男人看到的是

我和你都不曾使用过的一个身体。
天空湛蓝，矛盾于一个启示；
从悬挂的角度看，女人看到的是
我和你都不曾深入过的一个洞穴。

在大海的蔚蓝和天空的湛蓝之间
有一条线，却没有一点蓝的意思，
反而看起来像一根刚捆过海兽的绳索。
男人问女人：我是否真的存在？

女人问男人：你一生中做过的最疯狂的事情
是什么？不会是寻找真正的答案吧？
我和你，就是这样进入角色的。
没有例外，即便他们从未在悬崖边坐下过。

Life Roles Series

A man and a woman perch side-by-side on a railing,
the sea below, and the cliffs thirty meters high—
beyond their shadows, the sea is a deep blue,
roiling, and in that deep blue roiling, the man sees

a body neither you nor I have ever put to use.
The sky is a bright blue, contradictory with revelation;
from above, what the woman sees
is a cave neither you nor I have ever entered.

Between the deep blue of the sea and the bright blue of the sky
is a line, but there is no idea of blue there,
instead it looks like a cord that has just trussed up a sea creature.
The man asks the woman: Do I really exist?

The woman asks the man: What's the craziest thing
you've ever done? You're not looking for a real answer, are you?
And that's how you and I fall into our roles.
There are no exceptions, even if the two have never sat side-by-side on a cliff.

人之初丛书

第一课是早春的腊梅。
院子里就有好几株，但你想看更远的地方
还有没有更好看的。小眼睛的腊梅，
沸腾如花的泡沫；小手一碰，
颜色便艳如蜜蜡。你看得很投入，
小小的身体像涌起的浪潮。你的专注
就如同是一次对真理的引用。
而计划之外，幸福是一种节奏，
谁在冒险就好比谁更好奇。
我们来到河边，我为你捕捉
天气和情绪的混合物。你不需要那些乐器。
你要挖掘的是天性使然。你的假如我是你
是一次还原，甚至将微妙的万变
恢复成了爱的知识。我感觉到你的份量。
一天比一天更重，一天比一天更宽，
石堤下，河水荡漾着浑浊的美德。
是的。我不再担心这面镜子是否恰当。

Human Nature Series

The first lesson is the early spring wintersweet.
There are many in the garden, but you want to look further
to see if there are even prettier ones. Small-eyed wintersweet,
seething with flowerlike foam; touch it
and the color turns bright as beeswax. You stare at it,
its small body surges like the tides. Your concentration
is like a recitation of truth.
Apart from any plans, happiness is a kind of rhythm,
and the one who takes a risk is the more curious.
We come to the riverbank, and I catch
a mixture of the weather and mood for you. You don't need those
           musical instruments.
What you want to unbury is our true nature. Your imaginings of me as you
is a restoration, or even myriad subtle changes
that renew into a knowledge of love. I can take your measure.
Growing heavier day after day, wider day after day,
Under the stone dyke, the river undulates with muddy virtue.
Yes, from now on I won't worry whether this mirror is suitable.

野人学丛书

微妙到踪迹皆无。但面目依然可圈
可点。你独特于我。飞起来时,
没人能看见我们的翅膀在哪里?
其实,只要会飞,你就有机会微妙于
你很想摆脱一切。记住,老样子里有
本色的辩证法。白天,唯物,
原则上不照搬真理;晚上,唯心,
按黑白,讲究生活里到底能有多少情趣。
按起伏的次数统计迷宫活跃的程度。
最难忘的是你的另一面,
向左倾斜,只有花心才莫测。
替右着想,唯有天赋委屈最大。
一眼望去,你已被命运放大了四十倍。
你的头发就像从峭壁上垂落的藤蔓,
一个野人来不及细看,抓紧藤蔓,
向崖顶攀援而上。一转眼,微妙再次上演了。
记住,一旦非此即彼,谁都可能是野人。

Study of Primitive Man Series

So subtle there are no traces. Still the appearance is quite
laudable. You're distinct from me. When we fly,
can no one see where our wings have gone?
In fact, just by flying, you have a chance to be subtle
about everything you wish to cast off. Remember, your usual ways
have a dialectics of inherent quality. In the daytime materialistic,
and in principal never imitating truth; at night idealistic,
adhering to right and wrong, caring how much appeal life really has.
Counting the fluctuations to measure the activity of the maze.
What's most memorable is your other side—
leaning toward the left, only the hearts of flowers are unpredictable.
Considered from the right, only talent has a complaint.
Glancing down, you've been magnified forty times by fate.
Your hair is like vines hanging down a cliff,
a primitive man has no time to look carefully and grasps the vines,
climbing toward the top of the cliff. In an instant, subtlety again performs.
Remember, whenever it's either/or, anyone might be primitive.

超人学丛书

老磨坊曾令你感动。没有一种教育
能和那秘密的时光相比。这几张相片
照得都不错，最关键的几个迹象
都被抓拍到了。是的。被磨盘磨过的青春
仍是黑暗的，但是，相关的变形
已足够用来恢复我们的本来面目——
你曾年轻得像一株年轻的水杉，
挺拔而安静，但更多的时候是新鲜而挺拔。
没有一种动物能在我的世界里
追赶上你的脚步。单纯的世界单纯你
总是比我们的速度更复杂。你喜欢说：
你跟不上我。好的。我们就假定，
围着你转是世界存在的一个理由。
我会让一只年轻的狮子来说服我，
接着，我会听从一群大雁的白色的劝告——
我不需要改变，我只需要追寻。我们就假定：
我能在你追上你自己之前追上你。

Study of Superman Series

The old mill once moved you. No education
could compare to that secret time. The photos
were taken well, the key indications
are all in the candid shots. Sure, the youth milled by those millstones
is still dark, but the correlated shapes
are enough for us to recover our true colors—
you were once so young you were like a young dawn redwood,
tall but quiet, or more often fresh but tall.
There is no animal in my world
that can overtake you. An innocent world and an innocent you
are always more complex than our speed. You like to say:
You can't keep up with me. Ok. Let's assume
one reason the world exists is to revolve around you.
I'll let a young lion convince me,
and then I'll listen to the white counsel of a flock of wild geese—
I don't need to change, I just need to pursue. Let's assume:
I can catch you before you catch yourself.

野草将我在黑暗中缓缓放倒，
就好像需要治疗的，不是心灵的局限，
而是迷宫是否还积极。积极的迷宫
就像我中有你，并且不沾边乾坤
好比一个容器。如此，迷宫是否有趣
就变得关系重大。有趣的迷宫
不止是一次难忘的经历，它还是
一堵可靠的挡箭牌，挡住了很多射向你的箭。
你该学会神秘地感谢神秘的帮助。
我知道，你的命运绝不可能雷同到
我已走到人类的尽头。你不需要夸张
你我的底线。你知道，我刚从婚姻的废墟中
拎出了成捆的暗箭。垃圾的报复，
真是干得漂亮啊。损失超过了毁灭，
新寓言很快就会翻开激情史的死角啰。
再具体一点，损失甚至比微妙的失败还要神秘：
损失的，不仅是你有过多少纯洁的精力，
不仅是你还有多少宝贵的时间；损失的
是欲死欲仙，是无法弥补的黑暗中的胜利。

——赠清平

Contemporary Poetics Series

for Qing Ping

The wild grasses set me down slowly inside the darkness,
as though what needs to be treated isn't the limits of the mind,
but whether the maze is still active. An active maze
is like me containing you, irrespective of whether the cosmos
can be likened to a container. So whether or not the maze is fun
becomes important. A fun maze
is not only an unforgettable experience, it's also
a trusty shield, shielding you from all the arrows shot at you.
You must learn to use mysteries to thank mysterious aid.
I know your fate can never duplicate
the extremities of humanity I've encountered. You don't need to overstate
our bottom line. You know from the ruins of a marriage I pulled out
a quiver of stabs in the back. Garbage takes its revenge
in a lovely way. Loss surpasses destruction,
and a new allegory will soon create a blind spot in the history of passion.
Let's be more specific: loss is more mysterious than subtle defeat.
What's lost is not merely much of the pure energy you once had,
and not merely some of the precious time you have left. What's lost
is your desire, that irreparable victory in the darkness.

道德学丛书

如果需要的话，这故事
会有一个结局的。怎么又是蝴蝶？
能动而盲目，一路飞过底层，

浏览自然的奥秘，就好像重要线索
都是可以裁剪出来似的。看不见的锋利
就藏在它随身携带的小剪子里。

几种主要颜色都配齐了，
搭配得也很绝妙：一旦扇动，
首先活跃的，就是思想的舞蹈。

从运动到表演，美丽的小剪子，
肯定着非道德的极限。这时，
所有的背景已模糊在篱笆的背后。

Morality Series

If it's necessary, this story
will have an ending. Really, butterflies again?
Mobile though blind, always flying low,

surveying the mysteries of nature, as though threads of clues
can be snipped out. An invisible sharpness
is hidden in the little scissors they carry on their bodies.

A few primary colors are neatly matched,
paired so cleverly: each flap,
above all energetic, is a thought dancing.

From movement to performance, those lovely little scissors
affirm the limits of amorality. And in that moment,
the scenery blurs behind a bamboo fence.

底牌学丛书

就好像在此之前，没有人知道
冬日的阳光可以这样射进来。
不是万箭，不是丝弦，即将消失的
也不是阴影和目标是否曾伟大过。

无声的倾泻持续着，就仿佛光的瀑布
要把你带回给我。你是你的礼物，
但这一层天真，现在已没有人能够判断。
你安静得就如同一个鸟窝。

不再飞翔了，温暖的记忆就会向一株橄榄树倾斜。
换个姿势，倾泻的就是冬日的阳光。
顺着这角度，神秘的感恩组织起微妙的意志。
在流泪的太阳下，你翻看过我们的底牌。

Study of Cards Series

It's as though before now, no one knew
winter sunlight could burst into a room quite this way.
It isn't a million arrows or silken strands, and what's about to disappear
isn't the shadows or goals that once were so great.

The silent torrent continues, as though a waterfall of light
will bring you back to me. You are your gift,
but no one now can judge that level of innocence.
You are as quiet as a bird's nest.

No longer flying, warm memory will tilt toward an olive tree.
Changing position, what floods in is the winter sunlight.
Following that angle, mysterious gratitude forms a subtle determination.
Under a sun of tears, you rifle through the cards we've been dealt.

抵抗诗学丛书

这首诗关心如何具体，它抵挡住了十八吨的黑暗。
这黑暗距离你的胸口只剩下
不到一毫米的锋利。

于是，一种界限产生了。这首诗关心你我对根的感觉。
什么样的语言会如此扎根？
你知道，我曾对你说：根，不在寻根中。

你信赖过黑暗中的友谊吗？你愿意诗化身为根吗？
你知道，假如没有那种感觉，无论有什么意思，
都和你没有关系。这首诗就是想结束这种状况。

非常明确地，这首诗只想对根说话。
这首诗假定你有非凡的听力。它是谁写出的，并不重要。
重要的是，你已在秋天读到这首诗。

你不只是你。你还有一个责任，你是你我。
感谢汉语的奇妙让你我不只是你和我，
也要感谢每首诗似乎都包含有一个命运的动机。

这首诗关心命运的动机如何体现，就好像
你我不是我的黑暗。假如你还没有忘记运动，
你我就是根的面面观。你最近是不是一个人爬过很多山？

Resisting Poetics Series

This poem concerns how to be specific, it can hold off eighteen tons
      of darkness.
This darkness is separated from your chest by less
than a millimeter of a sharp point.

And so, a type of boundary is born. This poem concerns how we feel
      toward roots.
What kind of language will put down roots?
You know, I once told you: Roots aren't searching for roots.

Have you relied on friendship in the dark? Do you want poetry to transform
      into roots?
You know, if that feeling didn't exist, whatever that means,
it would have nothing to do with you. This poem intends to put an end
      to the issue.

It's obvious this poem only wants to speak to roots.
This poem assumes you have extraordinary hearing. It's not important
      who wrote it.
What's important is that this autumn you read this poem.

You are not only you. You have a responsibility—you are you and I.
Thankfully Chinese distinguishes we from you and me.
Thankfully every poem seems to include an intended fate.

This poem concerns how fate is actualized, and it seems
you and I are not my darkness. If you hadn't yet forgotten to move,
you and I would be an analysis of roots. Haven't you recently climbed
      many mountains on your own?

复活学丛书

一小时后，星光的样子
将会比你现在看到的，更迷人。
迷人的星光里，会有很多带着诱饵的长线
抛向理想的冲突。当你来到对岸，
现实已被做过手脚，你会遇到
一个足有十五米高的大钟摆：
刚刷过漆，上下泛着釉光，衔接工作
做得很巧妙。它摆来晃去，
就仿佛它要催眠的是站在你身后的
某个巨大的东西。按这样的比例，你像是
虎皮鹦鹉嘴上叼着的一枚扣子。
但是，你不渺小于我已掌握的任何真理。
这么多刺，这么多天真的流露，
但是，醒来，醒在何处，其实已无法选择。
这么多他人的血，从你的皮肤里
渗出来。新的综合鲜明你
有过一个思想的源泉。所以，你肯定听说过
我的名字叫红。请停止呻吟和尖叫。
一个谜就可以救你，假如你答应过
放聪明点的话。我想，我会做得比这些刺更好。
我会记住你的选择的。我的位置有天赐的一面，
和他们不同，我活在你我之间。

Resurrection Series

In an hour the stars
will be more incredible than what you see now.
In the enthralling starlight there will be a baited line
tossed into a conflict of ideals. When you arrive on the other bank,
reality will have been altered, and you will encounter
a fifteen-meter pendulum:
freshly painted, coated in a shiny glaze, with ingeniously made
linkages. It swings back and forth,
as though wanting to hypnotize some enormous thing
standing behind you. Based on its scale, you are
a button held in the beak of a budgie.
However, you're no more trivial than any of the truths I've grasped.
There are so many thorns, so many betrayals of innocence,
but whether and where you wake isn't a choice.
The blood of many men oozes
from your skin. A new synthesis displays
your source of ideas. So you've surely heard
I'm called Red. Please stop all your screaming and moaning.
A riddle can save you, if you respond
with a halfway clever answer. I believe I'll do better than the thorns.
I'll remember your choice. My position is partially predestined,
unlike the others, I live between you and me.

洗脑学丛书

从吹向四月的风中，截取
并制作出这音乐，既然你的名字里
飘着北京的柳絮，那也就没什么好隐瞒的。
欣赏完桃花，再欣赏喜鹊的小运动鞋。

枝条的每一下颤动，都会有一层无法洗掉的绿
渗向复杂的心理。如此，著名的洗脑
很容易被编入新内容。下面将要出场的是
语言和现实的双人舞。扭胯的语言

搂着挺胸的现实，转着快圈，
将整个现场介绍给道德的记分牌。
人不现实，比人太现实，更暧昧，
更多内部的消息，更诡谲于生命的张力。

A Study of Brainwashing Series

In the wind that blows into April, bringing
and creating this music, since Beijing catkins
float in your name, there's nothing to be hidden.
Admire the peach blossoms, then admire the magpie's tiny sneakers.

Every quivering branch causes an indelible layer of green
to ooze toward a complex psychology. And so, the well-known brainwashing
is easily given new content. What will appear below
is a *pas de deux* of language and reality. Gyrating language

holds onto square-shouldered reality as they spin,
introducing the scene to morality's scoreboard.
Impractical people are shadier than the overly practical,
full of inside information, turned cunning from life's tensions.

野花心理学丛书

野花能有多野？这条路
为什么这么奇怪？安静得就如同
还没有发作过的歌喉。你倾听得越久，
高贵的野蛮人留下的脚印越像是
一记响亮的耳光。那些被践踏过的栅栏
想必是记忆的特殊的记号，但是
很遗憾，你的记忆还从未使用过它们。
一旦展开，歌喉很容易就婉转成
起伏的思路。比如，在底线附近，
可能有过另一番情景：野花才不野呢！
声音很大，共鸣的野火里
像是有一桶水泼向了无边的肺腑。
再次出现时，你浑身透湿。
冒着烟的教训很呛人，很给旋律面子，
即便跑了点调，也很说明问题。
这些高原上的野花确实没有其他的秘密，
它们很大方，优美于你我有一种奇妙的才能——
就像玛丽安·穆尔早就提醒过的那样。

Wildflower Psychology Series

How wild can wildflowers be? Why is this road
so odd? It's quiet as
a throat that's never sung. The longer you listen,
the more footsteps left by noble barbarians
sound like a slap. The trampled fences
are presumably memory's special markers, but
unfortunately your memory has never used them.
Once opened, the singer's throat easily transforms
into a rippling train of thought. For example, somewhere near the bottom,
perhaps there was once a different scene: the wildflowers weren't wild!
The sounds were loud and resounded in the wildfire
like a bucket of water thrown over a bottomless heart.
When you reappear, you're soaking wet.
The lecture emits a choking smoke, gives the melody its due respect—
though it goes off key, it illustrates the problem.
These plateau wildflowers have no other secrets,
they're elegant, more graceful than this mysterious talent you and I share—
just like Marianne Moore once reminded us.

换骨学丛说

抵达之前，会有很多和解，
但不会有幸运。会有很多谜，或是
就不信谜不死你，但不会有
无法揭开的谜。谜是严厉的，
你真的需要我把每个环节都铺垫好吗？
为什么幸运不能太廉价？
因为它不抗震，至少这一回，
至少在这一点上，它没有对电视新闻说谎。
严厉的幸运或许才能带来
神秘的帮助。否则，即使脱了胎，
也别想换骨。你想知道换骨学的
政治底线在哪里吗？一个人的痛苦
就是宇宙的痛苦，但不是国家的痛苦。
一个人的痛苦只可能在国家和国家之间的
绝对的深渊里得到解决。时间能抹平的，
只是你我的结局或局限。时间能抚慰的，
你现在知道，诗会做得更出色。

Study of Changing the Bones Series

Before arriving, there will be many reconciliations,
but there won't be any luck. There will be many riddles, and though
superstitions won't kill you, there won't be any
unsolvable riddles. Riddles are serious,
must I really prepare each step for you?
Why doesn't luck come cheap?
Because it isn't quakeproof, at least this time,
at least at this point, it hasn't lied to the TV news.
Maybe only bad luck can bring
magical aid. Otherwise, even if you're reborn,
you can't change your bones. Want to know the political bottom line
of the study of changing bones? One person's pain
is the universe's pain, but it isn't a country's pain.
One person's pain can only be alleviated in the absolute abyss
between countries. What can be evened out by time
is simply the ending or limits of you and me. What can be comforted by time,
you know now, poetry can do better.

稻草人丛书

拍拍石头的肩膀，意思是，
你刚扎好了一个稻草人：你在它身上看到了
人的简陋。人的减法。制作它，只消耗了
半捆猪草。它的脊骨是用墩布把做成的，
两臂呆板如尺子。你从它身上想到了
人的丑陋。人的空心。但田野里的逻辑
会赐给它另一种美。金色的守望者
只是它的一个影子。你的记忆斗不过
它身上的风景。你要求它逼真，
将人的威权带进自然的轮回中——
你盼望它成为麻雀永远的对手。
而敌人的概念从来就很无耻，比无知更无耻。
于是，它替你出场，至少表面上是如此。
或者，它的回报已多于丰收，而你要寻找的东西
将会把我们引向奇迹的发生。

Scarecrow Series

When you pat a rock on the shoulder, it means
you've just put up a scarecrow: you see in his body
the crudeness of man. The subtraction of man. Making him only took
half a bale of pig-grass. His spine is a mop handle,
his arms are as stiff as rulers. His body reminds you
of the ugliness of man. The hollowness of man. But the logic of the field
will grant him another kind of beauty. The golden sentry
is merely his shadow. Your memory can't win against
the landscape of his body. You want him to be lifelike,
bringing man's authority into the cycles of nature—
you hope he'll become the eternal enemy of the sparrows.
But the concept of enemies is always shameless, more shameless than ignorance.
And so he takes your place, at least so it seems on the surface.
Or, what he gives in return is more than a harvest, and what you seek
will lead us toward something miraculous.

平衡术丛书

我母亲回忆说，我从小就不挑食。
她原先有很多证据，但现在她只记得
我喜欢啃筷子。按她的说法，我在筷子上留下的
痕迹就像一只会弹琴的小老鼠。有一阵子，
家里每个月都要更换一把筷子。
我不记得筷子的事。在失踪的时间里，
我只记得烤过的麻雀的小骨架子。
我的胃口很强大。我的脑海里经常浮现出
奔跑在宇宙深处的美丽的动物：
它们的脖子很干净，从未被圈套过。
它们的身材很适合语言的解放。
它们有你我没有的自我。它们出没在筷子
无法够到的地方。它们首先是我的动物，
其实是诗的动物。你很快会明白这一点的。

Equilibrium Series

In my mother's memories, I was never a picky eater.
At first she had sufficient evidence, but now she only remembers
that I liked to nibble on my chopsticks. According to her, I left marks
like a little piano-playing mouse. For a while,
we had to switch chopsticks every month.
I don't remember the chopsticks. Of those missing moments,
I only remember the skeleton of a roasted sparrow.
My appetite is enormous. Beautiful animals often appear
in my head, running through the deep recesses of the universe:
their necks are unblemished, they've never been ensnared.
Their shapes can easily be liberated by language.
They have a sense of self that you and I don't. They come and go
where chopsticks can't reach. They're my animals above all,
though really they're poetry's animals. You'll figure this out soon enough.

最基本的礼貌丛书

一大群雨燕来到了唯一中。
春天的唯一中，园林的唯一中。
没有人知道你为什么不这样说——
一群燕子飞进了唯一中。
它们把天空变成蓝色音箱，它们在生活之外
排演命运的偶然。它们的个头这么小，
它们的身手这么灵动，它们的游戏这么真实，
以至于你只是路过此地，并看到它们
在你的头顶编织一张快乐的毛毯子。
它们曾是最机灵的提词者，
它们记得所有被我们遗忘的台词。
快乐的见证。它们像小小的犁铧
将生命中的唯一匆匆掠过。一道道痕迹，
在记忆中变成一根根细绳。你被松绑的时候，
它们让淅沥的小雨变得年轻——
每一只燕子都代表一个秘密，
每一只燕子都整理过一条线索，
每一只燕子都欢乐过你的生命中
至少有过十七个春天的瞬间。
你是属于瞬间的人，所以，这些雨燕
才会来到了唯一中。它们的出场是一次兑现。

——赠林木

Basic Manners Series

for Lin Mu

An enormous flock of swifts arrives in a singularity.
The spring's singularity, the garden's singularity.
No one knows why you don't say it like this:
a flock of swifts flies into a singularity.
They turn the sky into a blue loudspeaker, outside life
they rehearse the randomness of fate. They're so small,
so agile, and their games so real
that if you pass by you can watch them
weaving a blanket of joy overhead.
They were once the most clever prompters,
remembering all the lines we've forgotten.
Witnesses to joy. They're like tiny ploughshares
hurrying through the singularity of life. The many traces
turn into many fine ropes in memories. When you're untied,
they turn the rustling shower of rain young again—
each swift represents a secret,
each swift threads a clue,
each swift has celebrated that your life
has had at least seventeen brief spring times.
You belong to a brief moment, and so these swifts
have come into the singularity. Their appearance is a sign of good faith.

原始权力丛书

来吧。向我们证实你是否真实。
现在的时机不错。我们把雾赶进了历史，
并在尘土上浇上了水泥。现场很光滑，
再没有影子能妨碍我们互相辨认。
我们出了大价钱，用语言制作了
一个坚固的瓶子。他们有断头台，
我们有神秘的瓶子。惩罚从瓶子开始，
世界是一副刑具。但我们想对你网开一面。
如果你真实，我们就会因你的真实而获得一次解脱。
我们并不在乎你的面目是否因真实而清晰。
一般情况下，我们不拿真理作筹码。
我们赌的是，你能用你的天才
改变恨的习惯。这里，舞台比宇宙还大——
如果你真实，我们就会感到一种痛苦。
我们现在只能用痛苦来衡量你是否真实。
来吧，向我们的痛苦证实你究竟有多少天才。
来吧，如果你有天才，真实的钩子
会照顾好这首诗的。请抓紧时间。

Primitive Power Series

Come on. Prove that you're real.
Now is the time. We stuff smog into history,
spread cement over dust. The scene is shiny,
no shadow will keep us from recognizing each other.
We've paid a high price, and used language to produce
a sturdy bottle. They have a guillotine,
we have a magic bottle. Punishment begins with the bottle,
the world is a set of torture instruments. But we want to give you a way out.
If you're real, we'll win our freedom with your reality.
We don't care if your features are distinct from being real.
In most cases, we don't use truth as a poker chip.
We bet that you can use your talent
to change hate's habits. Here, the stage is bigger than the universe—
if you're real, we'll feel pain.
Right now we can only use pain to judge whether you're real.
Come on, show our pain all your talent.
Come on, if you have any talent, the hooks of reality
will take care of this poem. Be quick about it.

新人生丛书

生活很复杂。于是，你听见
倒垃圾的声音。从黑塔似的楼顶
往下猛地一倒。从场面上看，幸存是风景——
这"本地的抽象"循环着你我。
一只野猫，毛发蓬乱，目光阴冷，
耸动着身体，将垃圾抖落在地上。
生活比人复杂："我是猫"就是一个经典的例子。
生活经常被揪送到狭窄的引号中——
那里，刺猬和喜鹊相遇在
无声的肉搏中，因替身而美丽。
至于人，人被扭送到引号中，
只是看上去像带了一副耳机。
生活比生活更复杂。一场生活比一种生活
听起来更无耻。如此，生活只属于
生活的一部分。就如同切开一个脐橙，
你用刀子把生活分成三瓣。你只取走了
其中的一瓣。你在精神的屏幕上留下了
刺猬的背影，你在生活的背影里
留下的是美丽的复杂。如此，
你只是属于你的生活的一部分。

New Lifetime Series

Life is complex. And so, you hear
trash being thrown out. Thrown down fiercely
from the dark peaked roof. At the scene, what survives is the scenery—
this "abstract locality" encircles you and me.
A feral cat, fur matted, eyes cold,
arching its back, shakes trash onto the ground.
Life is more complex than people: "I am a cat" is a classic example.
Life is often dragged into the middle of narrow quotation marks—
There, hedgehogs and magpies meet
in silent hand-to-hand combat, beautiful because they're stand-ins.
As for people, people are handed over to quotes
and look like they're wearing headphones.
Life is more complex than life. A lifetime sounds more brazen
than a life-kind. Therefore, life belongs
only to a part of life. Like slicing open a navel orange,
you use a knife to cut life into thirds. You've only taken
a third of it. On the mind's screen you leave behind
the shadow of a hedgehog, on the shadow of life
you leave behind a beautiful complexity. Therefore,
you only belong to one part of your life.

走出洞穴丛书

你走出洞穴。半小时前，在幽暗中
你有着一头成年棕熊的体重。
每个脚印，都是对大地的无知的肯定。
十分后，一个极限在洞口欢迎你。
阳光打在你的脸上，你的毛发像斑斓的呼吸。
你蜕变成一只崭新的豹子。变形记很尽职，
将你还原成一道野性的彩虹。
世界隐藏在肉中，于是你奔跑，
冲向一只小羚羊。你扑上去狠狠咬住
它的喉咙，将它掀翻在草甸上。
它的喉咙里回响着真理的哨音。
你不再需要洞穴。你需要大地的启示。
我觉得你的路线选得很有意思——
沿着你留下的踪迹，我也尝试着
走出我们的洞穴。我用羚羊的骨头
炖了一锅汤。放入沙枣后，果然很滋补。
不过，我的进展很慢，到目前为止，
只能说，与迷宫打了一个平手。

Leaving the Cave Series

You leave the cave. Half an hour earlier in the gloom
you were as heavy as a grown bear.
Each footprint is an affirmation of the ignorance of the earth.
Ten minutes later, a boundary welcomes you at the cave's mouth.
Sunlight hits your face, your hair is like multicolored breath.
You molt into a brand-new panther. The transformation records are dutiful,
and turn you back into a wild rainbow.
The world is hidden in flesh, so you run,
leaping at a tiny antelope. You pounce and sink your teeth
into its throat, flipping it down onto the pasture.
Its throat reverberates with a whistle of truth.
You won't need the cave again. You need the inspiration of the earth.
I find the path you've chosen interesting—
following your tracks, I also try
to leave our cave. I use the antelope's bones
to make a soup. I throw in some oleaster for nutrition.
But my progress is slow—up until now,
I've only managed a tie with the maze.

生命密码丛书

一路走来，四月比天上的白云
还要散乱。丁香胜过连翘，将人性一笔带过。
这么多小碎花，比漂白还白，
她们的呐喊就如同裹在旗袍里的斜塔。
万劫则像宇宙的小性子，幽怨荒原
已不再能说服历史。没有野火，
燃烧还能算风景吗？另一种可能是，
四月是最仁慈的月份。仅就北京而言，
你便可以找出一千个例子。发芽的自我
离你最近。但你太忙乱。脚下的泥土
踩上去咯吱作响。浮冰奏鸣曲
向时间推荐你的肖像权，裂纹越多，越美丽。
仔细一看，各种碎块多得就好像
你从未走出过废墟。废墟万岁。
闪念中已没有顽念，你已原谅唯有命运
是由不肯革命的事物构成的。
他们的命运如此。你的命运
也绝不会特殊过这首诗的命运。

Life's Password Series

The whole way, April scattered farther
than the clouds. Lilacs surpassed the forsythia, sweeping our emotions along.
So many broken blossoms, whiter than bleach,
the women's shouts were like a leaning tower wrapped in flags.
The ages are like the wayward universe, and a bitter wasteland
can no longer convince history. Without wildfires,
can burning still be called scenic? Another possibility is that
April is the kindest month. Even in Beijing,
you can find a thousand examples. There are germinating selves
all around you. But you're in too much of a hurry. The mud
groans underfoot. Sonatas of ice floes
recommend your portraiture to time, the more cracks, the better.
Looking closely, there are so many fragments it seems
you've never left the ruins. Long live ruins!
There's no stubbornness left in your thoughts, you've forgiven your fate
since it's made up of things that refuse to rebel.
Their fate is like that too. And your fate
won't be any more special than the fate of this poem.

奇迹政治学丛书

从无边的黑暗领回
这白鹅。它瘦了，但仍然很肥。
抱它的时候，就好像
你要把一台电视机抬到地下室。
它因你肯冒险而显得
比以前更漂亮。它也很幸运
因为你看上去像是知道
如何走出无边的黑暗。一路上，
它的屁股晃动如活跃的
晚报专栏。满天飞好不正经，
小道消息才不翻脸
你为什么要把它领回来呢。
它这么野，就仿佛
纯粹的自由不可用于
人和人之间的比较。
它是你的可爱的新娘，如果
你愿意等上一百年。或者，
如果你愿意给世界半小时，
它会像一个邋遢的证人，暗示
你和世界已有约在先。一环扣一环
也拿它没办法。给它冲个澡吧，
对它再好一点：把它当狗养，
对它说你对猫说过的那些话。
对它许诺，你的爱天真于
危险的心灵。对它发出更明确的邀请，
这种事，你不会再做第二次的。

Miraculous Political Science Series

Bring back from the boundless darkness
this white goose. It's thinner now, but still plump.
When you carry it, it's as though
you're hefting a TV down to the basement.
Because you're willing to take the risk, it appears
even prettier than before. It's also lucky
because you seem to know
how to leave the boundless darkness. On the way
it shakes its rump like a lively
evening news column. It's indecent to flit about,
yet the gossip doesn't turn hostile
about why you brought it back with you.
It's so wild it seems
pure freedom can't be used
to compare one person to another.
It is your lovely new bride, if
you want to wait a hundred years. Or,
if you want to give the world half an hour,
it will be a sloppy witness, a hint
that you and the world are already engaged. Time after time
you can't catch hold of it. Give it a shower,
and be good to it: raise it like you would a dog,
and tell it what you've told the cat.
Promise it your love is innocent
of dangerous thoughts. Give it an unequivocal invitation—
you won't do this sort of thing again.

友谊学丛书

你来自一个大陆。你身上
有沙漠的影子。无边的寂静
像一张药方，风把它吹到你的脚下。
你不会把它错看成是神的菜谱。
你的拿手戏是制造气氛，
向灵魂提供各种结构。
星期六下午，你会带着一瓶酒
去看望老朋友，而她已经变成鸽子，
居住在树洞里。以前，你从未想过
那么高的地方会有一个洞。
虽说每个人都有一个未来，
但是你，不会去主动选择未来。
你不会急于熟悉你的未来
就好像它无法促成一场伟大的友谊。
你把腌过的鱼翅放在
野猫蹲守的台阶上；它们
有时是五只，有时是三只。
它们的专注使你深受启发。
如此，你用巍巍雪山冰镇我们的孤独。
你咀嚼各种植物的根须，
你表现得很积极，就好像扎根扎对了，
可以不宿命。你租用了
一棵海棠的时间。所以，
你需要每天给我浇一次水。

Friendship Studies Series

You come from a mainland. Your body
carries the shadow of a desert. Boundless silence
is like a prescription the wind blows to your feet.
You won't mistake it for a god's recipe.
Your greatest skill is to create an ambience,
offering various structures to the soul.
Saturday afternoon, you bring a bottle of wine
to an old friend's house, but she's already become a dove
and lives in a hole in a tree. Previously, you never thought
that such a high place would have a hole.
It's said every person has a future,
but you won't pursue any one future in particular.
You aren't anxious to know your future
as though it will never become a close friend.
You throw the preserved shark fin
onto the steps where the feral cats lurk; sometimes
there are five, sometimes three.
Their attention inspires you deeply.
So you use the lofty snow-capped mountains to ice our loneliness.
You chew on the roots of various plants,
you seem energetic, like you've put down roots in the right place,
and nothing is predestined. You have rented
a begonia's time. Which means
you must water me once a day.

回声学丛书

西红柿疯了。现实全是对立面。
它想象一个影子从早到晚捏它身上的
没日没夜。它设想自己曾三次拒绝过
世界之最。它请主持人传达一个信息：
没有吃过疯西红柿的，请再举一次手。
但这一幕很快就会过去。很快，
它就嫌骨头炖得不够烂，还没烂到骨子去——
这么点火候都掌握不好，
要是遇到虚无和面具，该怎么办？
还能怎么办！如此，它嫌骨子里的矛盾
比宇宙还浅薄。它嫌鸡蛋还疯得不够。
说到底，扔出去的鸡蛋还是没有摆脱
理性的轨迹。鸡蛋比操蛋和法律还会装傻。
比绝望还自尊。它把自己投进
一口深井。它忽然想到列夫托尔斯泰
在《伊凡伊利奇之死》里漏掉的一个细节。
这口井，涉及了太多的比喻。
但愿黑暗王国不会弄错了。它想象自己
正在穿越黑暗王国的喉咙。记住，
饥饿本身并不构成答案，只有回声才是神圣的。

Echo Studies Series

The tomato has gone mad. All reality is antithesis.
It imagines a shadow is pinching its body's timelessness
all day long. It imagines it's rejected the extremes
of the world three times. It asks the MC to make an announcement:
all those who haven't eaten a mad tomato, please raise your hand.
But the scene passes quickly. Soon
it's annoyed that the bones aren't done, it hasn't cooked down to the bone—
the fire can't handle it,
if it meets with nothingness and masks, what will it do?
What can it do! So it's annoyed that the conflict of the bones
is shallower than the universe. It's annoyed that the eggs haven't really gone mad.
In the final analysis, the discarded eggs still haven't cast off
their rational orbits. Eggs can play dumb even better than bullshit and laws.
More egotistical than despair. It throws itself
into a deep well. It suddenly thinks of all the details Tolstoy
left out of *The Death of Ivan Ilyich*.
The well brings up too many metaphors.
Let's hope that dark realm doesn't go wrong. It imagines itself
crossing the dark realm's throat. Remember,
hunger itself doesn't constitute an answer, and only echoes are sacred.

秘密语言学丛书

忘掉那些废话吧。语言的秘密
神秘地反映在诗中。一只蓝樫鸟飞进诗中，
而天空并没有留在诗的外面。

你的秘密也反映在诗中，
你去诗中的湿地辨认美丽的鼠尾草；
而我，将会在诗中遇见你。

语言秘密地活着。活出了生命的
另一种滋味。语言因为等待你的出现
而听任太阳下有不同的生活。

你是它的植物。它这样选择你——
从生活的阴影中走出，你来到一簇绣球花前；
掀动草叶的风像一次治疗，而那些幽蓝的花瓣毫不避讳

语言的器官是否像它们一样精巧而漂亮。
你曾困惑于语言的器官不够鲜明，
现在，它们生动得就像你没有做过的一种爱。

下一步，你需要从生命的阴影中走出，
就好像语言的秘密取决于诗如何行动。
如果你选择飞，你的身上会长出靛蓝的翅膀。

Secret Linguistics Series

Forget that nonsense. Language's secrets
are mysteriously reflected in poems. A bluejay flies into a poem,
and the sky doesn't remain outside the poem.

Your secrets are also reflected in poems,
you dry out a poem's wetland and identify a lovely Japanese sage;
while I, I will find you in a poem.

Language lives secretly. It lives out life's
other flavors. Language waits for you to appear
and permits different lives under the sun.

You are its flora. It chooses you like this—
leaving life's shadow, you come to a cluster of pincushion hydrangea;
the wind rippling the grass is like a cure, and those dull blue petals don't dodge

the question of whether the organs of language match them in allure.
You once considered that the organs of language aren't distinctive enough,
but now they're as lively as a kind of love you've never made.

The next step is that you must leave life's shadow,
as though the secrets of language depend upon the behavior of poetry.
If you decide to fly, your body will grow indigo wings.

祖国学丛书

时间的教育完美于大地很经验，
它终于在我的内心结出一个果实：
神秘的是，祖国高于一切。
多少苦难暧昧于不走运，多少血的代价
淡漠于生命之轻，多少无名的光荣
惨烈于历史很游戏。当我寻找秘密的源头时，
我注意到了黑板。从黑板开始的，
不会在黑板上结束。黑板是祖国的眼睛——
我听了进去；值日时，我抢着擦黑板；用大脸盆接水，
从一楼抬到三楼。用力擦，一股牛劲
异样着我的小身板。清水很快浑浊，但这浑浊
滋养了我最初的幸福感。同时，这浑浊也很模糊，
就好像有个小东西被心潮推上了浪尖。
你还记得被心潮第一次启蒙时的样子吗？
为了捍卫我擦黑板的权力，我有时会用小拳脚狙击
潜在的竞争者。我也习得了堂皇的说理——
你们当中谁能把黑板擦举得比我高？
我有身高优势，能擦到你们够不到的地方。
美女教师偏爱我的说法，因为她是
我父亲的同事的妻子。她的表扬，现在听起来
也很有意思：经我之手，擦洗过的黑板乌亮得像黑镜子。
从镜子开始的，不会在镜子里结束。
与此相似的还有，从床上开始的，不会在床上结束。
从严肃的游戏开始的，不会理会死亡的可耻
和心灵的背叛。圈子好大啊，但是，
怎么绕，都绕不过依恋感。神圣而纯粹，
基本权利里应该有这些成分。这难道还需要
特别的假设吗？祖国很天赋，所以，我的问题是
你知道什么时候祖国是一个动词吗？

Motherland Studies Series

Time's education is completed by the earth's experience,
and at last it bears fruit in my heart:
what's truly mysterious is that our motherland outshines all else.
How much pain is turned ambiguous by bad luck, how much bloody cost
is dimmed by the lightness of life, how much unnamed glory
is made violent by history's games. When I search for the mysterious source,
I notice a blackboard. What begins with a blackboard
will not end on a blackboard. Blackboards are our motherland's eyes—
I hear it: when it's my turn, I insist on cleaning the blackboard
      with a large washbasin
I lug up from the first floor to the third. Rubbing forcefully, my small frame
warps with the effort. The water quickly turns dirty, but this dirtiness
nourishes my earliest happiness. At the same time, the dirtiness is uncertain,
like some small thing is being forced onto the tip of a wave by a surge
      of emotion.
Do you remember what it felt like the first time you were inspired by a surge
      of emotion?
To protect my blackboard-cleaning authority, sometimes I ambushed
potential competitors with my fists. I learned how to reason convincingly—
Who among you can get the blackboard eraser as high as I can?
I have the superiority of height, I can erase places none of you can reach.
A teacher liked what I said, the wife
of my father's colleague. Her praise now seems
telling: under my hand, the blackboard turned as dark and shiny as a black mirror.
What begins with a mirror will not end in a mirror.
Along those same lines, what begins in bed will not end in bed.
What begins with serious games won't understand the disgrace of death
and a heart's betrayal. The circle is very big, but
no matter how you move around it, you can't get past your longing.
      Sacred and pure—

我现在就有两个例子：当你想祖国一下时，
请不要感情用事。另一个是，
当我祖国时，那一切是如何成为可能的。

basic rights should be afforded that status. Does this really still require
some special assumption? Our motherland is gifted, and so my question is,
did you know 'motherland' is a verb?
I have two examples: When you want to motherland for a while,
please don't give in to your emotions. The other is:
When I motherland, everything somehow becomes possible.

纪念迪伦·托马斯丛书

小海湾纵容着生命的轮回，
每天如此，第一次涨潮已经退去，
第二次涨潮随时都会扑上来，将停车场淹没。
杨炼的宝马在那里已停了五个小时，
但从酒吧出来之前，没有一个旅游者
能意识到这险情意味着什么。

在两次涨潮之间，美丽的滩涂
就像是被天堂盖过的一个邮戳。
重新洗牌啰。这题材好得
几乎给每一种明信片都带来了运气。
潦草的苇丛上，海鸥的叫声听起来
就如同两只咖啡杯轻轻碰撞在了一起。

苍鹭的小单杠稳稳地架在泥地上，
想怎么练，就怎么练。不就是神秘
现在已变得异常迟钝了吗！宇宙可是
从来不知道什么叫吹牛。你体验过
必经之路上仍有中世纪的旧城堡
在那里撑腰的感觉吗？破壁连着残垣，

但每一寸，都透露出完整的尊严。
建造这城堡的人肯定死过不止一回。
人和人不一样，才有这小小的心得
像熏过的鲑鱼。黑暗中的美味啊，
你需要找到另一张嘴，才能明白我说的
生活的滋味并不全部来自生活本身。

In Commemoration of Dylan Thomas Series

The small bay is winking at the cycle of life—
every day is like this, the first tide has already retreated,
and the second might rise any moment, swallowing the parking lot.
Yang Lian's BMW has been parked there for five hours,
but before they come out of the bar, none of the tourists
realize what this dangerous situation implies.

Between the two tides, the beautiful beach
is like a postmark stamped by heaven.
Reshuffle the cards. The subject matter is so good
it brings nearly every postcard good luck.
In the tangled weeds, the seagulls' cries sound
like two coffee cups lightly clinking.

The thin horizontal bars of the herons are planted solidly in the mud,
training however they like. How the mysterious
has become strangely sluggish! The universe
has never known how to boast. Have you ever experienced
that feeling of the only possible path being flanked
with medieval castles? Tumbledown walls against broken-down sides,

each inch revealing an intact dignity.
The people who built these castles have died more than once.
People are not all the same, and so there is this tiny bit of knowledge
like smoked salmon. A scent in the dark,
you must seek out another mouth to understand when I say
life's flavor doesn't only come from life itself.

纪念保罗·克利丛书

认识你是因为罪。一个线条丰腴的女人，
你画下了她。这也许是重新认识世界的一次机会。
一个女人就能解决全部的问题。至少，你曾这么设想过。
要么就是，你曾处理过这样的灵感。
你决定让她不穿衣裳，躺在树杈上。
而在以前，她只习惯躺在沙发上，或床上。
你做了一个伟大的艺术家能做的事情——
仅仅是改变背景，就改变了一个人的未来。
那年我十六岁，因为读《红字》而没有完成
数学作业，因为读《呼啸山庄》而发现
自我是可以改造的，因为读《理智与情感》而陷入
白日梦，而移情就是用苍蝇拍敲打《忏悔录》；
如果有真相，如果你真想了解的话，
那么，是巨大的诱惑充实了我。那也是
我第一次认识到我的身体并不完全属于我。
我反抗，于是又意识到我的身体
经常不在我的肉体里。在三四米之外，
我的身体会变成一棵枣树。院子里有两棵树，
一棵是枣树，另一棵还是枣树。
这不是废话，这是一种节奏练习，
牵涉到你究竟想把世界摆在什么地方。
直到现在，仍是诱惑在充实着我。
所以，我的情况和他们不太一样。
每隔八年，我都要引用一次你的话——
我多么想谦卑地跪下来，但跪在谁的面前呢。

In Commemoration of Paul Klee Series

I know you because of sin. A woman of buxom lines,
drawn by you. This might be a chance to know the world anew.
A woman can solve any problem. At least, you once imagined that.
Or one could say you once dealt with such inspiration.
You decided she would be naked, reclining on a tree limb.
In the past, she was accustomed to lying on a couch or a bed.
You did what great artists can do—
simply by changing the background, you changed a person's future.
I was sixteen that year—I read *The Scarlet Letter* and didn't finish
my math homework. I read *Wuthering Heights* and realized
that a self can be constructed. I read *Sense and Sensibility* and fell
into a daydream, where empathy beats out *Confessions* with a flyswatter.
If there's a truth to it, and if you really want to understand,
it's that I was enriched by a deep temptation. It was also
the first time I noticed my body doesn't entirely belong to me.
I resisted, whereupon I noticed my body
frequently wasn't inside my flesh. Three or four meters away,
my body could become a jujube tree. There were two trees in our courtyard,
one was a jujube, and the other was also a jujube.
This isn't nonsense, it's a kind of rhythmic practice,
which leads to where you actually want to put the world.
Today, it's still temptation that enriches me.
So my situation is different from theirs.
Every eight years, I quote something you said—
I want to kneel down with humility, but whom shall I kneel before?

在爱与死之间，我发明了
这安静。这绝对的空间。它的地平线上
停放着一台褪色的轿子。花的轿子，
峭壁的轿子，无底洞的轿子。如果只是人去，
不可能留下这样的空。风吹着暗红的流苏，
就仿佛永恒被揪住了小辫子。
我发明了我的死，但我不确定
诗歌的战士是否打搅到了你。我多少感到抱歉，
我选择了永恒的失败，而不是浅薄的胜利。
这里确实很安静。云的白毛巾
刚刚擦洗过一片柿子树。小池塘里
反射着雨水激发的新的光泽。跳舞的芦苇
给你曾抵制过的思想松了绑。在野鹅带来的友谊里，
姿态一番，你不会被问及莫名其妙。
不是大地本身，而是大地的孤独
确定了这礼物，它甚至珍贵到令基调准确。
像你一样，在此之前，我曾无数次想过
我的死，但不曾描绘过它。
现在，我开始描绘我的死，指出它
在爱与死之间有过一个确切的位置。

In Commemoration of Lü Yuan Series

In between love and death, I invented
this peace. This absolute space. On its horizon
rests a faded palanquin. A palanquin for flowers,
a palanquin for cliffs, a palanquin for bottomless pits. If it were merely
      the departure of a man,
it wouldn't leave behind this emptiness. A wind rustles the red tassels,
as though eternity has been caught by its small braid.
I have invented my death, but I can't be certain
if poetry's soldiers have disturbed you. I feel somehow apologetic
that I've chosen eternal failure instead of superficial success.
It really is peaceful here. The white towels of clouds
have wiped the persimmon trees clean. The small pond
reflects a new luster set off by the rain. The dancing reeds
loosen the fetters of thoughts you've resisted. In the friendship of wild geese,
with a change of position, you won't be baffled by questions.
It isn't the earth itself, but the earth's loneliness
that chose this gift, so valuable it brings everything back in tune.
Like you, before this I thought countless times
of my death, but had never described it.
Now, I begin to describe my death, pointing out
it's had a set position between love and death.

追忆丛书

列车缓缓启动。世界模糊成背景。
只有美丽的自我箭在弦上。
还有谁发出的声音
会比靶心被击中时更响彻呢？
列车驶向平原以南，
平原安静得就像一大片膏药，
听任钢铁的速度将随意的涂抹
变成神秘的愈合。加速之后，
列车驶向上海，驶向青蛙作为订婚礼物的国度，
驶向记忆比空气更多的江南小镇，
驶向太平洋深处的情人节。
你靠在车门上，全然不知
有一个世界正随你而去，被你扩大到
天真的极限。该死的天真，
假如天真无助于机遇。十分钟，
你有点后悔。毕竟，天真纠正过命运。
但是在另一个时间里看到
现在的时间的真相，这似乎不是
所有的人都能习惯的事。
酝酿出自内心的真实：还有谁的记忆
会如同这慢慢旋动的瓶塞？
还有谁能在孤独中判断出这区别的含意：
我的记忆总能轻易地追上时间，
而你的记忆从来就没追上过时间。

Remembrance Series

The train starts up slowly. The world blurs into a backdrop.
There is only the beautiful inevitability of the self.
Will someone's voice
reverberate more than a bull's-eye when struck?
The train heads south of the plains,
and the plains are so silent they're like a swath of ointment,
allowing the casual spread of the steel's speed to turn
into a mysterious form of healing. After its acceleration,
the train heads to Shanghai, to a nation where frogs are engagement gifts,
to little southern towns where there is more memory than air,
to a Valentine's Day deep in the Pacific Ocean.
You lean against the train doors, completely unaware
there is an entire world following you, and you've expanded it
to the limits of innocence. This damn innocence,
as though innocence never aids opportunity. Ten minutes
and you're a bit regretful. After all, innocence has redressed fate before.
But seeing the truth of this moment
at some other moment, that seems to be something
not everyone can.get used to.
A truth brewed in the heart: who else's memories
will be like this slowly turning cork?
Who else in their loneliness can judge the meaning of this difference:
my memories always easily catch up to time,
while your memories have never caught up to time.

变速器丛书

寻找生活的对应物时，以前用过的
那些装备已不再有用。
抛物线不抛物，而是直接将你
射进一片黑暗。凡原始的，
才最接近政治。凡陋习的，
非魔术一番不可。凡不可改变的，
直接交给钉子。叮叮当，

人生几何响当当。这里，很显然
对应还不是对称。新轨道反光
审美有点反动。向月亮看齐，
生活几乎对应于人生。
向秘密看齐，会委屈谁呢？
反正不会是你我。宇宙的身份
不仅没有降低，而且它愿意

这样解决你遇到的问题：
飘渺已不同于虚无。一颗樱桃的
飘渺，足以对付虚无的变戏法。
一只蝴蝶的飘渺，可以让任何化身
失去轻重。不再需要化身时，
意味着一种进步。是有点可耻，
但它毕竟缩短了人和文明之间的距离。

沿化身而迷惑，怎么说，
也不如沿替身而聪明于困惑。
但是，沿转身而一再委婉，这真的好于
放任人和人之间的现有距离吗。

Transmission Series

Searching for the counterpart of existence, this used equipment
can no longer be used.
Parabolas aren't parabolic, but shoot you straight
into the darkness. Ordinary primitiveness
is the closest to politics. Ordinary corruption
couldn't exist without magic. Hand over to the nails
what ordinarily can't be changed. *Bang bang*

this brief life blares out. Here, the clear
parallels aren't symmetrical. The new orbit's reflected light
is a bit aesthetically reactionary. Juxtaposed with the moon,
existence nearly corresponds to human life.
Juxtaposed with secrets, who can feel wronged?
Not you nor I, anyway. The status of the universe
not only isn't reduced, but it's willing

to solve a problem you've encountered:
indeterminacy isn't the same as nothingness. A cherry's
indeterminacy is enough to counter the conjurings of nothingness.
A butterfly's indeterminacy can make any incarnation
lose its weight. When no further incarnation is needed,
a kind of progress is signified. It's a bit shameful,
but in the end it shortens the distance between man and culture.

Incarnations and confusions—how to put it—
aren't as good as substitutions and intelligent puzzlement.
But are turnabouts and constant tact really better
than not interfering with the distances that exist between people?

我的迷惑是美妙的意义可被美妙地制造，
人的破产，似乎好像大概暂时
还无法全面地造成一种心灵的腐败。

你的困惑是，假如我不是替身，
那么你是谁？一条鱼的飘渺
如何决定现在的味道？再比如，
一朵花的飘渺如何插足
没大没小。或者，用你熟悉的例子，
怎么魔术，一枚枫叶的飘渺可染红
百年孤独中的这一天。

I'm confused about how beautiful meanings are created beautifully—
the bankruptcy of man seems fairly temporary
and can't devise the absolute corruption of the soul.

What puzzles you is, if I'm no substitute,
then who are you? How can the indeterminacy of a fish
determine this flavor right now? Or another example,
how can the indeterminacy of a flower be involved
in impudence toward one's elders? Or, to use an example you know,
how can the indeterminacy of a maple leaf magically dye red
this single day, amidst a hundred years of solitude.

随着那新鲜的深度协会

——纪念谢默斯·希尼 (Seamus Heaney 1939–2013)

爱尔兰的爱。足够遥远
但绝不陌生。每一次挖掘，
爱尔兰的兰，都会随着
那新鲜的深度，在孤独的语言中
找到美妙的支撑。深绿的叶尖摇动
一个细心。动摇的花蕊
在这样的口风中，会如何看待
人生的片面，已成为诗的俘虏呢。
至于挖掘留下的坑，只有汗水
才能填满。也只有这样的坑，
才能在时世的艰难中加深一次信任。
给倒影打一个电话吧——
既然它们已在风景中的风景里
坚持了这么久。爱是冰。
不信的话，你可以自己动手试一试。
八月的最后一天，像一头大象。
别这么看着我。我现在是个盲人。
这样的底线，就该有这样的盲人。
德尔默·施瓦茨，即"洪堡的礼物"中
洪堡的原型，他悲伤地说过——
"接触是一杆枪"。情况的确很严峻，
但是你，坚持掀开油腻的铁匠铺门帘，
教会我像铁锤一样，去信任每一次触摸。

After the Society for New Wisdom Association

In memory of Seamus Heaney 1939–2013

The love of Ireland. Far enough
but not unfamiliar. With every dig,
Ireland's orchids follow
that new wisdom, and find in the language of loneliness
a supreme support. The deep green tips of leaves sway
the careful heart. How will the pistils trembling
in a tone of voice regard
this side of human life, now poetry's prisoner.
As for the hole left by the digging, only sweat
can fill it. Only this kind of hole
leads to a deeper trust in this difficult world.
Call the reflections—
they've already persisted this long
in a landscape set in the landscape. Love is ice.
If you don't believe it, you can see for yourself.
The last day of August came like an elephant.
Don't look at me that way—for now, I'm blind.
Blind men for dark times.
As Delmore Schwartz, Humboldt's model
in *Humboldt's Gift*, painfully said—
"For like a gun is touch." Everything is grim,
but still you open the blacksmith's oily shop curtain,
teach me to be like a hammer, to trust in every touch.

人在佛蒙特，或比雪白更寓言入门

北纬45度，雪统治了背景；
怎么左右，都绕不开从东到西；
白色的秩序仿佛在提前排练
现实和自然的界限终究会在何处消失。
但看样子，绿头鸭并不怎么介意，
它们选择了就地越冬，
又一次，将南方封存在未知中；

凡风景比自然更原始的地方，
都会频繁闪现这些野鸭的身影，
就好像它们正在给沉寂的群山暖场；
天敌已彻底消失，它们从积雪的
坡岸上，扑进冰冷的河水，
为你示范冬泳的秘密——
就好像冷，依然是最好的秘诀。

四周，阿巴拉契亚的山峰多到
只有这奔流的基训河记住了
你的名字；仿佛不如此，
时间的遗忘就无法触及我们身上
更隐秘的正义。其他的迹象
还包括：被拔光了叶子的枫树
一头扎进北风的祈祷。

乌鸦的叫声如同单飞的颂歌
频频点缀世界的边界。
瞒过了天使，将冰之心均匀到露骨的
雪，陈列着自己的裸体，
令大地看上去像半个替身。

In Vermont, or a More Allegorical Than 'White as Snow' Primer

At 45 degrees north, snow dominates the background;
whether to the right or left, you can't get around going east to west;
the sequence of whiteness seems rehearsed
and the boundary between reality and nature eventually dissolves.
But it seems the mallards don't mind,
they choose to spend their winter here,
sealing the south up in the unknown again;

Each spot with scenery more primitive than nature
flashes with the silhouettes of those mallards,
like an opening act for the taciturn mountains;
their natural enemies entirely gone, they flap down
from the snowbanks into the freezing river,
demonstrating the mysteries of winter swimming for you—
as though coldness is still the real secret of success.

All through the Appalachian highlands
only the fast-flowing Gihon remembers
your name; it doesn't seem that way,
time's forgetfulness can't touch the hidden justice
in our bodies. Other indications
include: a maple tree plucked bare,
a prayer struggling into the north wind.

The crows' caws are like a lone ode
ornamenting the boundaries of the world.
Deceiving the angels, they distribute ice-hearts evenly over the barefaced
snow, and display their own nakedness,
making the earth look like half a body-double.

一抬腿，就是尽头。一尽头，
人的极度的孤独便是你的极端的长处。

回过神来，清冽的星光犹如
一种私人签名，把你的目光
远远带向宇宙的另一面。
请不必担心我们如何返回，
月光下，还从未有过一种遥远
比你身上的小涵洞
更抵近我们的起源之谜。

As soon as they lift a leg, it's all over. And when it's over,
you excel at extreme solitude.

Recovering, the chilly starlight is like
a personal signature, it carries your vision
to the other side of the universe.
No need to worry how we'll get back,
beneath the moonlight, there's never been a distance
closer to the riddle of our origins
than your body's small tunnels.

枫糖液入门

整个下午，本地的枫糖液
扭动着琥珀色的腰肢，
从各种陌生的角度，
向你兜售一击甜蜜的老拳；

如何出手，难道还需要
用时间的政治把你的眼睛
再蒙上一次吗？靶子是现成的，
一直都隐藏在你身上；

即便明确成对象，也是彼此
较着劲，比客观还漂亮。
唯一需要解释的是，这里，
老，究竟涉及怎样的含义。

剔透到浓稠，但它并没隐瞒
这树蜜是从高达四十米的枫树上
采集来的；而那些开凿在树干的小洞，
作为甜蜜的通道，它们的历史

已有一千六百年。仅凭这一点，
它已指出，你的记忆存有怎样的缺陷，
且亟待通过这些蜜液的注入，
才能重返荒野中的停留——

那里，经过原始的消化，
甜蜜的暴力仿佛已练就了
一种绝对的分寸，足以从内部
将你直接唤醒到纯粹的原型之中。

Maple Syrup Primer

That whole afternoon, the local maple syrup
wriggles its amber figure
and from many angles of unfamiliarity,
it hawks its sweet fists at you.

To fight back, must you really
hide your eyes with the politics
of time? The target is ready-made,
it's been hidden in your body all along.

When it becomes a clear target, it offers
a match of wits, prettier than objectivity.
All that must be explained is: here,
old has its own connotations.

From shiny to sticky, it doesn't conceal
that the sap was collected from maples
forty meters tall; as for those little holes carved into the trunks
as paths of sweetness, their history

goes back sixteen hundred years. This alone
shows the shortcomings of your memory,
only through the pouring of this syrup
can one return to the wild—

and there, with primitive digestion,
the violence of the sweetness practices
a perfect restraint, and so, from the inside, it is enough
to awaken you to your pure original form.

雪色人生入门

两幢房屋分别坐落在
小基训河的两边，都听得见
河水的声音。蛋黄色的那幢
用于失眠，辗转心曲，以及探索
人熊之间的底线心理学；

乳白色的那幢用于工作，沉思，
疏通诗歌的下水道，努力克服
比白夜还时差，将蔓越莓茶喝成
咖啡的瀑布，以及不管时机是否合适，
也要放飞心巢中每一对想象的翅膀。

那突然萌生的，且一旦萌生
便无法逆转的，不断增强的，
被牵动的，不受天气好坏影响的，
返回的感觉，就这样悄悄
绷紧在两幢山区的房屋之间。

从睡觉的房子走向工作室，
怎么着都不像外出，反而更像
一种返回，甚至连距离都很合适；
从工作室出来，碧蓝的晴空
如同心灵的魔术；接着你穿过

小桥冬天的耐心，走向那座
比睡眠的颜色还要乳黄的
临时居所，这返回犹如一条捷径——
就仿佛整个事情已明显到
只有在别的迷宫中，你才需要出口。

Snow-Colored Life Primer

Two buildings separated
by the two banks of the Gihon River, both
hear the rush of the water. The yolk-colored one
is for insomnia, the heart that tosses and turns, and an exploration
of the basic psychology between bears and people;

the cream-colored one is for working, thinking,
dredging out poetry's sewers, trying to deal with
the perpetual daytime of jetlag, drinking cranberry tea
into a waterfall of coffee, and, whether or not it's the right moment,
setting free every pair of imaginary wings from the heart's nest.

And that suddenly conceived,
irreversible once thought, steadily increasing,
easily influenced, unaffected by the weather
feeling of return
is quietly stretched out between these two houses set in the hills.

Walking from the house where we sleep to the office,
it doesn't seem like going out but instead always seems
like a return, and even the distance is right;
leaving the office, the cloudless blue sky
is like a clever slight-of-hand; after you cross

the winter endurance of the little bridge, and walk toward
that temporary residence even more butter-colored
than insomnia, the return seems like a shortcut—
and everything is so clear it appears
you'd need an exit only from some other maze.

基训河入门

两旁的白雪应该是它
刚刚脱下外套，长裤和披肩——
就好像关键时刻，唯有你的赤裸
能令人生的虚无稍稍收敛一下
那古老的敌意。陌生的纬度中
有纯粹的维度，它凭借清晰的倒影
忠实于你原来的确有机会
安静于世界的秘密。岸上，
高大的乔木静静地撑开
仿佛和它无关的，碧蓝到
辽阔的呼吸。转念一想，
本地的抽象中，唯有它甘愿
自觉地低于人的目光——
但这难道不恰恰是它精通于
将你从我们身上吸引过去的证据吗。
或者，面对它不知疲倦的流淌，
敢不敢和大地也赌一把：
将你的孤独锤炼成更精准的技艺。
绝对的冷，有可能依然是
一种礼物：就好像时间需要玩具时，
它送去的是数不完的，有着锋利的
边缘的冻雪，尺寸犹如
从史前巨兽嘴里敲碎的牙齿。

Gihon River Primer

The snow on either bank must be
the jacket, pants, and cape it's just stripped off,
and it seems that at the moment of truth, only your nudity
can cause the emptiness of life to gradually restrain
that ancient enmity. An unfamiliar latitude
has unadulterated dimensions, it relies upon distinct reflections
to keep to your original opportunity
to stay silent about the world's secrets. On the banks,
a giant tree silently unfurls
a vast blue breath
that doesn't seem to belong to it. Reconsidering,
in the abstraction here, only it is willing
to realize it's beneath people's attention—
but isn't that proof of how good it is
at drawing you away from the rest of us?
Or, facing its indefatigable flow,
do you dare bet against the earth:
temper your loneliness into exacting artistry.
Absolute cold is perhaps
a kind of gift: it seems when time needs a toy,
what it sends can never be counted, with a sharp
edge of icy snow, whose dimensions
are like the great gnashing teeth of prehistoric animals.

威悉河畔入门

感谢时差。感谢被颠倒的黑白
在陌生的时光里激起了
新的浪花。存在就是迟到。
最好的存在，就是最深的迟到——
就如同我们只配相遇在
我们的偶然中。想弥补的话，
得首先看看附近有没有
可以和捷径媲美的渠道。
感谢捷径。肉体曾是此岸的
最明显的标志；而现在，
因为这沉重的水花，肉体也是
彼岸的阵地，且真实于
我们有时会喃喃自语：到头来，
唯有孤独的灵魂是可信赖的。
感谢在我们中间，这些水
曾如此抽象，又如此及时；
以至于我们确有可能
比我们的碎片，更完整地
漂浮在生命的记忆之中。

——赠李栋

Banks of the Weser River Primer

for Li Dong

Thankful to jetlag. Thankful to inverted dark and light
in an unfamiliar time, for stirring up
new waves of experience. To exist is to arrive late.
The best existence is utmost lateness,
just as we encounter each other only
in our fortuitousness. If you want a remedy,
first you must look around
for a path that rivals a shortcut.
Thankful for shortcuts. The flesh was the shore's
clearest symbol; but now,
because of this heavy spray, the flesh is also
a battlefield on the other shore, and stays true
to what we sometimes mumble to ourselves:
in the end, only a solitary soul can be trusted.
Thankful that in between us, these waters
were once this abstract, and this timely
so much so that we may float even more completely
than fragments of ourselves
in these recollections of our lives.